D0949725

THE HAPPY STEPCOUPLE

THE HAPPY STEPCOUPLE

How Couples with Stepchildren Can Strengthen Their Relationships

RACHELLE KATZ

ROWMAN & LITTLEFIELD
Lanham • Boulder • New York • London

Published by Rowman & Littlefield
An imprint of The Rowman & Littlefield Publishing Group, Inc.
4501 Forbes Boulevard, Suite 200, Lanham, Maryland 20706
www.rowman.com

6 Tinworth Street, London SE11 5AL, United Kingdom

British Library Cataloguing in Publication Information Available

Library of Congress Cataloging-in-Publication Data

978-1-5381-3064-3 (cloth)
978-1-5381-3065-0 (electronic)

∞™ The paper used in this publication meets the minimum requirements of
American National Standard for Information Sciences—Permanence of Paper
for Printed Library Materials, ANSI/NISO Z39.48-1992.

CONTENTS

v

INTRODUCTION

The Happy Stepcouple is designed to help couples with children from prior relationships thrive despite the complexity of stepfamily life. As you know, it isn't easy to form a relationship that doesn't begin with a clean slate. In fact, the number of issues you and other stepcouples juggle (financial constraints, ongoing conflicts with former spouses, disagreements about parenting styles, among many others) can make it downright challenging—especially since you may have had to face them before you and your partner had the chance to learn how to work well as teammates.

Because of the number of challenges stepcouples encounter, it probably won't surprise you to learn that they experience **three times more stress** than couples in first unions, and the stress is so intense that more than **two-thirds break up** within the first few years of committing to each other.[1] This accounts for far more relationships than you might imagine.

In the United States, more than 42 million adults have married more than once. While it is not known how many of these remarriages form stepfamilies, estimates indicate that approximately two-thirds of remarried women are biological mothers or stepmothers, and about half of this group resides with stepchildren.[2] This accounts for millions of women, and this figure considers only those who are remarried. Many more stepcouples choose to live together without being married, as cohabitation has become a more common alternative rather than a precursor to remarriage.

As the number of stepcouple relationships continues to multiply each year, so does the number of those that are short-lived. This is a problem of epidemic proportion that must be addressed since everyone in a family suffers when these relationships end.

There is some good news: if stepcouple relationships last longer than five years, the odds of staying together greatly improve. Even better news? By learning how to strengthen their emotional connection with each other, most stepcouples can withstand the trials and tribulations of stepfamily life and thrive within it. *The Happy Stepcouple* is a comprehensive and practical guide that will show you how.

This book is unique. Other self-help books focus on ways to overcome specific stepfamily challenges, such as boundary violations and insider/outsider issues (problems created when one partner is excluded from the inner family circle). Unfortunately, resolving these problems is only half the battle of restoring harmony between partners since it does not address and repair the real reasons why these relationships fail. *The Happy Stepcouple* offers a revolutionary approach to overcoming stepfamily problems and strengthening a stepcouple's bond by examining the two primary reasons why so many of these relationships get in trouble. Want to know what these are, and what you need to do to prevent this from happening to you?

In my opinion, stepcouples experience problems because partners fail to understand, agree to, and fulfill each other's unspoken needs and expectations. First, when expectations do not match up to one's reality, each partner becomes frustrated and disappointed. Second, the way they then communicate about their feelings inadvertently increases each other's insecurity levels, damaging the most important ingredient in a relationship—feeling safe and secure with each other. Both of these factors fray emotional bonds far more than the specific problems the couples encounter.

THE GENESIS OF *THE HAPPY STEPCOUPLE*

This project is a continuation of my interest in and work with stepfamilies. Though I had been a licensed marriage and family therapist for several years, I only became aware of the unique challenges facing stepfamilies when I married my husband, who at the time had a four-year-old daughter. I believed, like many others, that over time our family would be indistinguishable from traditional ones, and I was surprised that my attempts to create an inclusive, loving home were met with such difficulty. I wondered if I was doomed to feel like an outsider forever and blamed myself for my family's inability to blend.

At the same time, I began to work with other stepmothers in my psychotherapy practice. I observed a common thread: just like me, they joined their new families with lots of enthusiasm, energy, and dedication but quickly became exhausted and depressed after failing to integrate their new families. While they understood it would take time to form a new family, they weren't prepared for the task to prove impossible. They blamed themselves when family members didn't bond, and a pervasive sadness overtook their lives.

To better help these stepmothers overcome their depression, restore their self-esteem, and create happy families, I began researching stepfamilies, in general, and stepmothers, in particular. Only a limited number of books were available on this topic, so I decided to conduct my own research. I created a website called *Steps for Stepmothers* that included a space where stepmothers could give each other support and advice. To obtain more in-depth data, I asked them to fill out a lengthy questionnaire. To attract stepmothers, I advertised my new site on Google. Incredibly, more than 3,000 stepmothers answered the questionnaire within the first year, and another 3,000 filled it out by the second! From this research and from my experience as a psychotherapist and stepmother, I wrote *The Happy Stepmother* to share what I learned. I hoped that stepmothers would realize the title of my book does not have to be an oxymoron.

After *The Happy Stepmother* was published, I sponsored workshops for stepmothers and their partners. It quickly became apparent that stepmothers were not the only family members who needed help. Their partners also lived with fears, anxieties, and insecurities. They were wracked by guilt that they inadvertently harmed their children by getting divorced. They were also scared that their children would be unwilling to spend time with them if they imposed too many rules in their home. These concerns interfered with effective parenting and caused problems in their new relationships.

The stepcouples who attended my workshops were kind people who were doing their best under difficult circumstances. They loved each other very much yet were overwhelmed by their families' challenges. Even though each stepcouple had different problems with which to contend, they shared many of the same feelings: they were afraid the damage to their relationship was beyond repair, and they felt dispirited at the prospect of another failed relationship.

I knew through my work that most couples just need help strengthening their emotional connection with each other and that there were practical solutions they could use to support each other more fully. I started this book to help them do so. I began by researching books and articles in the fields of social psychology, communication, parent education, and marriage and family therapy. I also developed a new comprehensive online questionnaire designed specifically for stepcouples in order to gain as much subjective data as possible. I asked participants to share information about their problems and how they handled them. I also asked for their suggestions to help other stepcouples with similar problems. More than 1,275 people completed questionnaires in only a few months. The results provided me with a greater understanding of stepfamily life and an appreciation of the determination, devotion, and commitment stepcouples need to form new families. I am so grateful to all the participants who gave their time and effort and who were willing to disclose intimate details of their lives with frankness and honesty.

Survey participants shared that they experienced six major problem areas:

1. Dealing with their former partners
2. Juggling finances
3. Parenting stepchildren who have academic, behavioral, or interpersonal problems or who are emotionally distant or disrespectful
4. Navigating boundary issues
5. Working through differences in parenting styles
6. Facing insider/outsider issues

I will give examples of these problem areas throughout the book along with suggestions for diminishing their negative impact on your life. To protect everyone's privacy, I have changed names and modified certain details about the couples I describe. Please also note that for ease of writing, I alternate male and female pronouns by chapter, but in all cases the material relates to all genders.

THREE STEPS TO A STRONGER RELATIONSHIP

To help build a strong, loving relationship, *The Happy Stepcouple* offers three steps, each encompassing a section of the book. The first step involves examining and recalibrating the cultural expectations most stepcouples believe they must adopt in order to have a successful family. The second step is communicating with your partner in ways that instill confidence that you'll be at each other's side forever. This section of the book highlights the importance of feeling safe and secure in a relationship and provides exercises to help you develop more security. Lastly, the third step is learning how to deal with the most common stepcouple problems in ways that bolster each partner's security level. Together, these three steps can help you build and maintain a solid relationship. Let's break them down a little further.

Step 1: Revise Unrealistic Expectations

Many couples struggle to live up to an idealized vision of what they think family life should be. When they can't achieve that vision, they feel disappointment and frustration. Fights then ensue, and the way couples handle these conflicts can threaten the longevity of their relationship. This section will show you how to avoid that trap. You'll learn to

- identify and discuss your expectations of each other,
- understand the importance of reaching a consensus on the roles you adopt,
- recognize and accept that a "good enough" stepfamily can be successful and fully functional,
- carve out quality time with your partner,
- establish an open and fair financial arrangement with your partner, and
- redefine your role as a stepparent.

Secure couples don't have fewer problems than others. Nor do they work harder than other couples to solve their problems. But they do know how to demonstrate kindness, affection, and support to each other. They value and cherish their relationship and make it a priority. They focus on working on solvable problems and ignore those they cannot resolve. They know how to discuss sensitive issues without making each other feel inadequate. They also know the importance of creating positive experiences together. They have fun together during their leisure time and set aside time to go on dates. These seemingly small, everyday behaviors give their relationships strength that helps them endure and survive hard times.

Step 2: Improve Communication

Though love is fundamental to starting a romantic relationship, surprisingly, feelings of safety and security are needed to sustain one for the long haul. To explain why partners feel either safe or unsafe with each other, *The Happy Stepcouple* analyzes stepcouple relationships through the lens of attachment theory and helps you improve your communication by understanding and modifying your emotional attachment styles. Attachment theory is a concept that examines different ways that infants form attachments to their primary caregivers, and how these differences shape the way adults think about, behave, and communicate in relationships. Notably, attachment theory addresses how adults respond to partners during conflicts. Some of us tend to react in a secure manner while others respond in an anxious or avoidant manner. The clash of attachment styles during disagreements can exacerbate each of our insecurities and make us wonder if we can trust our partner to be on our side. Heightened insecurities weaken partners' bonds with each other—often to the extent that the relationship fails.

To help you feel more safe and secure in your relationship, *The Happy Stepcouple* provides several confidence-building exercises to boost your security level, techniques to reduce angry and other defensive feelings that impair your ability to listen to your partner during fights, and ways to modify outdated beliefs that limit your intimacy with your partner. It also provides a set of communication tools and "buffering techniques" to utilize during conflicts to prevent your partner's security level from diminishing. These practices will enable you and your partner to overcome the damage caused by clashing attachment styles and strengthen your emotional bond. You will be able to create a relationship that becomes a circle of safety from which to ward off dangers together. This section will help you

- understand how the "stepcouple shuffle" affects your relationship,
- identify your predominant emotional attachment reaction,
- recognize your partner's and your communication pattern during times of conflict,
- learn how to boost your level of security,
- learn how to increase your partner's feelings of safety and security during conflicts, and
- improve communication with your partner during conflicts.

Step 3: Address Your Specific Stepcouple Challenges

Lastly, we examine how secure partners deal with common stepfamily problems—including insider/outsider issues, jealousy, boundary violations, and power imbalances—in ways that promote kindness, compassion, and respect. From these examples, you can extrapolate ways to most effectively deal with your challenges. This section will help you

- learn how to do the "waltz of intimacy,"
- identify and overcome insider/outsider issues in a secure manner,
- soothe your partner's jealousy,
- establish healthy boundaries with family and friends, and
- share power equitably with your partner.

CAN YOU BENEFIT FROM READING THIS BOOK?

Let me ask you a few questions about your experience in your stepfamily:

- Do you and your partner argue so much about stepfamily issues that it interferes with having fun together?

- Do you and your partner struggle to compromise when making decisions?
- During times of conflict, do you and your partner feel like adversaries?
- Do you and your partner spend too much time criticizing each other?
- Does your relationship feel unbalanced? Does one of you have more control?
- Do you work so hard in your stepfamily that you have no time for other activities?
- Do you frequently resent your partner?
- Have you thought about ending your relationship?
- Do you and your partner no longer feel safe and secure with each other?

If you answered yes to just one question, you can improve your relationship by reading this book. It will give you evidence-based ways to revise unattainable expectations, learn how to handle conflicts, improve your communication, and build trust in each other. Armed with this knowledge, you will be able to successfully face any challenge your family may encounter.

HELP IS ON THE WAY

I bet you and your partner are exhausted from dealing with and arguing about problems in your stepfamily and need an emotional reset to let go of negative emotions caused by past arguments. *The Happy Stepcouple* will help you replace negative feelings with positive ones.

There is never one simple fix to any one problem. This is especially true for stepfamily challenges. Each stepfamily is composed of different people of various ages, related to each other through diverse lineages. Your stepfamily has specific problems that require their own tailor-made solutions. I will present you with many suggestions throughout this book. Implement the ones that are most relevant for your situation.

By applying small changes to your life, you can create a healthy, loving partnership. Let's begin your journey of healing.

Step 1

REVISE UNREALISTIC EXPECTATIONS

1

STEPFAMILY FALLACIES

Our expectations play a powerful role in all aspects of our lives. They shape our career goals and influence our choice of friends. Our self-esteem is largely based on whether or not we live up to the expectations we set for ourselves. We form an impression of partners from our notions of an ideal relationship. If, for example, you believe couples should spend all of their leisure time together, then you will be upset if your partner plays golf with friends every Sunday. However, if you think couples should spend some time apart doing things they individually love, then you will feel fine when your partner spends an afternoon doing so.

Most of us accept our expectations and the emotions they produce without question. We don't consider how large a role they play in our experience of everyday life, whether we are content or distressed. While some of our expectations are realistic, others are merely ideals that are hard to achieve, setups for disappointment and frustration. In the next few chapters, we will examine your expectations for your stepfamily, for your relationship with your partner, and for your role as a parent. Let's begin by examining how some common stepfamily expectations create problems for many of us.

Several unrealistic expectations trip up many stepcouples. The most destructive one is that successful stepfamilies need to "blend" and be indistinguishable from traditional families. Another is that stepparents must love their stepchildren as much as their own. And some stepparents believe they must fill the role of parent when their stepchildren spend time with them, a role that their stepchildren may object to and resist. These expectations are based on myths—not on reality.

I bet you have really tried to meet your expectations about stepfamily life and are exhausted and frustrated. Striving to achieve an impossible goal is wearisome and, ultimately, a waste of valuable time. The truth is, by reframing your expectations to make them attainable and by redefining your role in the family, you can create a happy, thriving family life. The more aligned our expectations are with reality, the more content we are.

WHAT SHOULD A STEPFAMILY BE?

Expectations of your stepfamily should not be shaped through the lens of traditional families. Stepfamilies are different—no better or worse.

As you know, stepfamilies are extremely varied. There are those with stepfathers, those with stepmothers, and those in which both partners are stepparents. Stepfamilies can be composed of either heterosexual or same-sex couples who are married or who live together. Children can live in a stepfamily full time, split their time between their parents' homes, or visit one parent's home occasionally. Stepfamilies can include members of multiple races and multiple religions and can consist of several generations.

Despite the unique nature of stepfamilies, most of us automatically accept that all stepfamilies should blend over time to become similar to traditional ones. We believe we just need to swap old partners for new ones who then will fill the same roles as our former partners. We expect that family members eventually will mix together harmoniously, similar to a choir whose voices meld in synchrony.

But in our quest to blend, we never stop to question if the traditional family is even ideal. As we know, many traditional families aren't as happy and functional as we imagine, and thus we are striving for something that is more romanticized than real. More important, we set ourselves up for disappointment by trying to become just like traditional families because the ability to blend is not entirely in our own control—it depends on stepfamily members' openness to forming relationships with each other. What's more, stepfamilies *are* different—comparing our families to traditional ones is like comparing the proverbial apples and oranges.

THE EXPECTATION TO BLEND

Blending has become the benchmark of stepfamily success. Those who have attained this status can boast about it, while those of us whose members mingle like oil and water can feel like failures. We would be far happier if we changed this benchmark to something that better reflects the true nature of stepfamilies. We could then celebrate in our stepfamilies' uniqueness.

You might wonder where the widespread belief that stepfamilies should look exactly like traditional ones came from. The mental health community popularized this concept to replace the negative connotations associated with the word "step." Just think about how stepmothers have been portrayed as wicked and evil for centuries. By adding "blended" to our cultural lexicon, the community hoped that stepfamilies would no longer be perceived as inferior to traditional ones. This relabeling was based on the best of intentions, and it was a long-overdue attempt to give stepfamilies equal status to traditional ones. Unfortunately, it isn't a realistic or accurate label, and it has caused many stepfamilies to feel as though they have failed. Listen to what respondents to my online questionnaire had to say about it:

> *I foolishly thought we could blend. The word is a misnomer. We are less blended now than 10 years ago.*
> *We are surely not the Brady Bunch!*
> *It is so much more difficult than I ever imagined.*
> *We are like two separate families living in the same house.*
> *We haven't bonded with each other's children as I'd hoped.*

Barriers to Blending

While a few stepfamilies do find the harmony of the "traditional family," the way most form prevents total blending. Stepfamilies come together after some or all of their members suffer losses and changes due to divorce or death, and it takes time to grieve and adjust to any loss. Some family members find it hard to move on from this painful time, and all it takes is one person to feel angry, sad, or resentful to prevent an entire stepfamily from blending. Here's one example.

Ava, a new bride, was very concerned that her new stepfamily was doomed to fail because her husband's ex-wife had no interest in meeting her. She wondered how she could build a loving relationship with her stepson if his mother would not acknowledge her. She didn't understand why his mother would refuse to meet her, a person with whom her child spent 50 percent of his time. After all, Ava was not responsible for the breakup of her husband's first marriage—she hadn't even met him until a few years after his divorce.

Ava wasn't expecting to become friends with his ex-wife, but based on both personal and cultural expectations that stepfamilies should blend, she believed they needed to develop an amicable, cooperative relationship to best care for her young stepson. I explained to Ava that blending might not be the healthiest or most desirable option for her family if her stepson's mother could not behave civilly in Ava's presence. Her stepson might be spared the unnecessary stress of witnessing this tension, as ongoing conflict between parents is very harmful to children.

I asked Ava to think about the traditional families she knew. How many of them seemed happy and functional? How many were dysfunctional? She quietly considered this question for several minutes and said maybe one-third to one-half were functional. I then asked why she was worried that her marriage would fail when at least half of the intact families she knew did not measure up to her standard and yet they stayed together. If she were to include all traditional families—from fully dysfunctional to fully functional—in her comparison, she might not be so nervous hers would fail.

I reassured Ava that blending is not a prerequisite for happiness. She could be very happy in her stepfamily without a relationship with her husband's ex. In fact, many stepmothers would consider her lucky that she didn't have to deal with an ex, many of whom can be intrusive and troublesome. It took Ava a little time to accept that her family was not going to fit into the idealistic model set forth by society. When she did accept this, she was no longer embarrassed and felt more secure in her relationship.

The dynamics between former partners are just one reason why stepfamilies may struggle to blend. Like anything else in life, timing matters. Stepfamilies form at different times of members' lives—some form when children are young, some when they are teenagers, and some when they are fully mature and living on their own. Stepfamily members may not share the number of experiences needed to form deeper attach-ments. It's not that some stepfamily members don't like each other—they just don't know each other.

This is a real issue for many children who split their time between two households after their parents' divorce. Spending a limited amount of time in one place can make it difficult, if not impossible, for them to form close relationships with all family members. One man named Jayson described his experience to me:

> *It was a huge adjustment when my dad remarried. I had to adjust to a dif-ferent neighborhood, different house, a different room, different rules, and a different life. My life was turned upside down. My dad was now spending more time with his new wife and her kids than he was with me. He adjusted to the changes much more quickly than I did, probably because he saw them on a daily basis and I only saw them four days a month.*

Eventually Jayson grew accustomed to spending time in this new household. He didn't mind that his father formed a closer relationship with his stepmother and her children than he had with them. He just wanted to make sure he and his father stayed as close as they had been when he was younger. So Jayson suggested to his father that they go out to dinner by themselves every so often. His father loved this idea, and they made a bimonthly ritual of going to their favorite barbecue restaurant together.

Spending only a little time with stepparents is just one reason why stepchildren resist close relationships with them. They may dislike the changes in their routines and lives brought upon by their parents' di-vorce or a death, and they may be less than enthusiastic when their par-ent commits to a new partner. They may fantasize that their parents will get back together and resent their stepparent for preventing this dream from happening. Even adult children whose parents have been divorced and remarried for decades may still hope their parents will reunite and thereby keep their stepparents at arm's distance.

Other stepchildren maintain an emotional distance from their step-parents because they believe all relationships are temporary and fragile, and they don't trust their parent's new relationship will last for very long. They don't want to get close to a stepparent and then suffer another emotional loss when the relationship breaks up.

Some stepchildren feel very protective of their biological parents, in particular their mothers, and believe they are betraying or rejecting them if they form a close relationship with their stepparents. Stepdaughters, in particular, resist bonding with stepmothers.[1] In addition to feeling intense loyalty to their mothers, they can feel competitive with their stepmothers for their father's affection. They may interpret their stepmother's activities, such as cooking and cleaning, as taking their place in the family and, consequently, develop hostile feelings toward her.

In a landmark study, researchers interviewed 1,400 families of divorce and studied them for almost 30 years.[2] They found that only 20 percent of stepchildren felt close to their stepmothers. Another longitudinal study of 20 years found that only about one-third of adult children thought of stepmothers as parents.[3] Half regarded their stepfathers as parents. These findings emphasize just how rare blending is.

Stepparents themselves may also struggle to develop strong, close relationships with their stepchildren, particularly when they see them only every other weekend or less. Their stepchildren may seem more like guests visiting the household than family members. Let's be completely honest: some stepparents are not entirely open to relationships with their stepchildren. They may be jealous of the time and attention their partners bestow upon them, resent the extra work they must undertake for them, or find their stepchildren's resemblance to their other parent to be an uncomfortable reminder of their partner's past.

The Pressure to Love, and Be Loved by, All Stepfamily Members

Adding to the pressure of trying to blend your stepfamily, you may believe you must love your stepchildren as much as you love your partner. Your partner also may expect you to love his children and vice versa in order to be a happy and well-functioning stepfamily. This expectation may be too difficult for most stepfamilies. While it may be possible for some stepfamily members to love each other, it's not a universal experience, and certainly not necessary for stepfamilies to thrive. Stepfamily members don't need to love each other; however, there's one, simple fundamental rule for all of us to follow: be kind, considerate, and respectful to all family members, including biological parents.

Do you feel guilty that you don't love your stepchildren? Do you feel you must keep it a secret because your family and friends will judge you if they know how you feel? If so, know that you are in a big boat—many stepparents are wracked by guilt and shame that they don't love their stepchildren as much as they think they "should" despite treating them with great care.

It may be just as challenging to develop close relationships with extended stepfamily members. Take in-laws for example. You may resent them for maintaining close ties with their ex-daughters- or sons-in-law for the sake of seeing their grandchildren. They may resent your presence in their son's or daughter's life and resist getting to know you. Or they may be older and not have the energy for or interest in getting to know you. These feelings may not change, nor do they have to in order to have a happy stepfamily. You can compensate for the emotional distance you feel with certain family members by seeking out other relatives or neighbors with whom to form closer ties.

HOW DO I REFRAME MY EXPECTATIONS?

There are two steps to take to adjust your expectations of your stepfamily: first, redefine what success means, and second, accept that "good enough" is pretty great. Let's explore how to go about these.

Redefine Success

Blending is a myth. Understanding this, stepcouples should redefine success as a family that is kind, respectful, and considerate of each other; one that gets to know each other slowly over time; one that forgives stepped-on toes and acknowledges complicated emotions. The best thing about this definition is that it's within your reach.

Readjusting your expectation to blend is an important first step toward accepting your stepfamily. Eliminating the word "blended" as a descriptor of stepfamilies from our cultural lexicon could really help too. What other word could replace it? In England, stepfamilies are called "extended" families, but in the United States we use this term to refer to cousins, aunts, and uncles, so we can't use that.

An alternative may be "hybrid," which describes a combination of different things, or "bi-nuclear," which Dr. Constance Ahrons coined to describe stepfamilies as having two centers, adjacent to each other but with acceptable differences between the mother's and father's houses.[4] This term does not create any expectations for the functioning of stepfamilies; it merely describes the architectural structure of stepfamilies as two distinct entities parallel to each other. Just like the "stepfamily," binuclear families include everyone: ex-partners, ex-in-laws, stepcouples, biological children, and stepchildren.

For many years I've mulled over adjectives to replace "blended." Of all the ones I've considered, "regenerated" is my favorite. "Regenerated" is defined as "to be formed or created again, to be spiritually reborn or converted, or to be restored to a better, higher, or more worthy state" (Merriam-Webster's, 11th ed., s.v. "regenerated"). "Regenerated" describes stepfamilies without imposing judgment or expectation on them. For the remainder of the book, I am going to refer to stepfamilies as regenerated.

Try this exercise: Every time you find yourself using "blended," replace it with one of the alternative expressions that most resonates with you. By substituting one word, you can begin to change your expectation about how stepfamilies should function, in general, and feel much better about yours, in particular. You can let go of feeling guilty that your stepfamily does not measure up to unrealistic cultural norms.

Accept That "Good Enough" Is Pretty Great

Once you've put aside this unrealistic expectation, the next step is to accept your family for its own unique qualities. Strive to accept your relationship with your stepchildren, in-laws, exes, and others as "good enough."

This is a difficult concept for most of us to accept at first. You may balk at this suggestion, just as a stepmother who attended one of my workshops did. Leila was offended by my recommendation she accept a "good enough" relationship with her stepdaughter. She wouldn't accept being "good enough" in any area of her life that mattered to her. While she did not excel at everything she undertook, and experienced obstacles, setbacks, and hardships in her life like everyone else, she believed hard work resulted in positive outcomes. She assumed that by being kind, loving, and considerate to her nine-year-old stepdaughter, she would develop a warm, loving relationship with her and create a happy regenerated family. Leila was very hurt that her stepdaughter's loyalty to her mother kept her at arm's length, and she considered ending her relationship with her partner because she didn't think she could tolerate feeling rejected for the rest of her life.

I told Leila it might be impossible to overcome the forces that prevented her stepdaughter from getting closer to her. Still, they could have a "good enough" relationship. By establishing "good enough" as her new expectation, she could let go of the pressure she was putting on herself and leave room for the relationship to grow and evolve naturally. Over time, Leila realized that "good enough" didn't mean she was necessarily giving up or resigning herself to a subpar relationship. As with other friendships she'd developed, she realized that an intimate relationship with her stepdaughter would develop naturally at its own pace, rather than being forced into existence.

Try this exercise: Do you need to accept that you can have a "good enough" relationship with one of your stepfamily members? Every time you feel sad about this relationship, remind yourself that it is "good enough" and that you can choose to accept your situation for what it is.

"Good enough" relationships may improve over time. Stepchildren and in-laws can change their attitudes toward you. You may appreciate new aspects of your stepchildren as they grow. By keeping an open mind about what your future looks like, you may be pleasantly surprised with what unfolds.

2

EXPECTATIONS OF
YOUR RELATIONSHIP

Much of our happiness and contentment is based on whether or not our expectations of regenerated family life are met. Our expectations of partners, and theirs of us, play as big a role, if not bigger, in determining how happy and content we are with each other. Unfortunately, most of us never give a second thought to exactly what we expect from partners, nor recognize the subtle influence culture, religion, race, and socioeconomic background play in shaping each of our expectations, and how differences between partners can lead to misunderstanding and negatively impact our relationships.

Unspoken and unfulfilled expectations cause frustration, unhappiness, and resentment. The trouble is, we expect a lot from partners: we expect them to satisfy our needs for intimacy, support, stability, happiness, sexual gratification, and more. While we can now derive more satisfaction from relationships than ever before, these expectations make us more vulnerable to disappointment. To avoid misunderstandings between you and your partner, it helps to be aware of the expectations you have for each other and to then discuss and clarify which ones are attainable and which ones need to be modified.

EXPECTATIONS OF EACH OTHER

I became aware of the importance of spelling out expectations early in my marriage. In passing, my mother-in-law asked me what I cooked for dinner on weeknights. Since I worked until 8 p.m., truth be told, I didn't cook dinner. I told her I heated up prepared food or ordered takeout. Her question made me wonder if my husband expected me

20

to cook our meals. When I asked him, he said he hadn't really given it much thought, but he had expected I would cook two or three nights a week. I was quite surprised that I hadn't been meeting his expectations. Quickly I explained that it wasn't possible for me to cook on weeknights unless I stopped working evenings, which wasn't an option for us financially. As we talked, my husband realized that his expectation was unrealistic and clarified that he didn't care if I cooked as long as we didn't spend too much time deciding what to eat. In the past, we could spend up to 30 minutes deciding which restaurant to order from, and he didn't like eating too late at night. Nor did I. Since I didn't mind the responsibility of choosing our meals, I offered to buy food during the day that would be ready to heat up when we came home. I was so grateful my mother-in-law asked me this question, because it prompted a conversation that, if we hadn't had it, may have caused us both irritation down the line.

Similar to many couples, my husband and I shared several expectations that we wanted each other to abide by. We wanted each other to be respectful, faithful, and kind. We also wanted each of us to work hard so we would be financially secure in the future. Before making any major decisions, we wanted to discuss them. And we wanted each of us to be committed to our marriage for the long haul.

Expressions of Love

As part of our conversation about our expectations of each other, we talked about our definition of love, notably how we expected to express and receive it from each other. My husband is a doer. If I ask him to help me fix my computer, for instance, he does it immediately. He sees this act of service as a way of expressing his love. I am more of a procrastinator, and if he asks me to go to the dry cleaner, I can take some time before picking up his shirts. This is not my way of expressing love. Instead, I am more apt to express my love by telling him several times a day how much I love him, or by grabbing his hand or massaging his neck.

These differences may seem minor, but they matter. It's easy for stepcouples to run into trouble when one partner expresses her love without really knowing if that particular way is meaningful to the other. For instance, you may value acts of service and spend hours making an elaborate dinner for your partner on Father's Day. Your partner, on the other hand, values togetherness and may not appreciate that you spent all day preparing the meal because he'd prefer to have spent the day with you. Or you might buy your partner an expensive gift because you like to receive tangible reminders of being loved. You might be disappointed if he or she isn't as thrilled with the gift as you had hoped. Your partner would have preferred a back rub. These differences are easily rectified once you share your preferences with each other.

Gary Chapman differentiates five primary ways that couples express love to each other: verbal expressions, quality time spent together, acts of kindness, physical affection (including sex), and gifts. How do you want your partner to express love to you? How does your partner want to receive your love? Here's a hint: we tend to express love in the way we want it expressed to us.[1]

Everyday Expectations

After discussing our preferences for giving and receiving love, my husband and I talked about how we expected to share our everyday lives. We found we had very different views about unexpected visitors. My husband wanted family and friends to be able to "pop over" at any time, whereas I wanted them to call first. He was raised in an apartment building that was also home to two sets of aunts, uncles, and cousins. His relatives entered each other's apartments without knocking. I grew up in a two-family home with my paternal grandparents living below. They always called before visiting us, and as an adult, I expected this from family and friends. While I love company, I prefer to have a few minutes to straighten up before a guest visits our home—especially because it is very easy for small city apartments to get messy. My husband understood my desire and agreed to have family and friends call first.

Wouldn't you know it, though? We have become friends with many of our neighbors, some of whom ring our buzzer without calling first. Even though we gently remind them to call first, they forget, and I have grown to accept that they will see our mess. This shows how important it is to be flexible at times and understand that household rules may be broken. Even so, I appreciate that my husband tried to protect my need for privacy.

My husband and I talked about many other everyday expectations that we had for each other. You and your partner may want to discuss these as well. Here's a list that may help:

- Sleep patterns: Do you expect to go to sleep together or separately?
- Eating patterns: Do you expect to eat meals together or separately?
- Intimacy: How often do you expect to have sex?
- Religion: Do you expect to attend religious services together?
- Pets: Do you expect to have pets, and if so, who will be responsible for their care?
- Neatness: How often do you expect to tidy up?
- Privacy: How much time alone does each of you need?
- Socializing: How often do you expect to socialize with family and friends? Do you and your partner prefer to only do things together as a couple, or is it acceptable to maintain separate friendships and activities?
- Decorating: Who will make decisions about decorating your home or apartment?
- Exercise: Do you expect to exercise together or separately? Do you expect that you and your partner will stay in shape throughout your relationship?
- Health and illness: Do you expect that you and your partner will take care of each other when ill?
- Household tasks: Do you expect that you and your partner will divide household responsibilities equally?

These topics are just a sample of the wide-ranging expectations we have of partners. You may come up with many more relevant ones to discuss with yours so you can clarify any differences you may have and decide how to deal with them.

Household Tasks

One of the main reasons so many stepcouples fight about household chores is mismatched expectations. Taking care of a household is a big job, and tasks must be divided between partners. Some couples sit down and spell out each of their responsibilities, while others let them evolve more organically. I didn't spend much time thinking about what household tasks I wanted to do when I married my husband. I immediately pitched in by cooking, cleaning, and arranging activities for us. You too may have thrown yourself headfirst into activities you believed you were supposed to do when you began living with your partner, without considering whether you had any other options.

Like many other stepparents, you may have taken on many chores for several reasons: to help out your partner, to become more integrated into your family, and to be accepted by your stepchildren. But you may have found that doing household tasks isn't the most effective means of developing a warm, loving relationship with stepchildren. In fact, most children don't pay attention or appreciate what is done for them until they are adults doing these tasks for their own children. Your partner may not have appreciated your efforts as much as you had hoped, and your frustration and resentment may tax your relationship.

Melanie, a stepmother, described her relationship this way:

When I married my husband, I wanted to be a super stepmother and super wife. I wanted to do everything for my stepson, preparing nutritious yet tasty meals for him. I wanted to give him lots of love and support without stepping on his mother's toes. I asked for very little, and I didn't complain when my husband refused to get a babysitter so we could go on a date for a couple of hours or when he would wander off with my stepson, forgetting I was with them. I would hold back from expressing my discontent, and when some small incident would happen, I would blow up, enraged that my needs were ignored. My husband would be shocked by my outburst and promise to do things differently. Unfortunately, he had limited follow-through. After an outburst, I would feel terrible I lost control of my temper, and retreat back into my role of super stepmom and super wife. This lasted until I realized this pattern was making both me and my husband miserable.

Melanie's experience is very common. You may have gone through this as well. If so, you have inadvertently set yourself up to be a martyr by taking on too many household tasks, creating an imbalance in your relationship. By working too hard, you've set a precedent that it's acceptable for your partner to do less, and you are left exhausted and unfulfilled. Eventually you will feel burned out and become resentful, particularly if your partner does not acknowledge or appreciate your efforts. Over time, the disparity between what you do and what your partner does will create an emotional barrier between you.

To prevent this, think about redistributing your household tasks equally. Make a list of what has to be done and then mark the tasks you do in one colored pen and the ones your partner does in a different color. You may realize your partner is doing more than you have given her credit for. If this is the case, express your gratitude for what she does. If your lists are not fairly distributed, consider rebalancing them. Eliminating just one task from your daily routine can make a big difference in helping you feel more relaxed and balanced. At first, your partner may resist making a change because it will give her an additional task. In time she will understand it's not fair for you to be overly burdened.

A note of realism: while equity is important in relationships, it's not always possible or practical to split tasks 50/50. Sometimes one partner is away from home and cannot do her fair share. If it's just not possible for you and your partner to split household tasks evenly, consider picking ones that fit into your life and interests. For example, your partner may choose to cook dinner every night because you have a long commute home. You may choose to garden because you love nature and your partner is allergic to pollen. Then you may feel like the tasks in your relationship are more fairly balanced between you and your partner.

EXPECTATIONS OF YOUR TIME TOGETHER

All of us expect and want to spend quality time with our partners. Unfortunately, our lives can be crammed with so many responsibilities that we often feel like business partners rather than romantic ones. Caring for children and/or working hard to support the family can exhaust us so much, by the end of the day all we want to do is sleep. A frequent complaint of many who completed my survey was that their sex lives had dwindled appreciably after a few months of living with their partners.

Many stepcouples expect that their lives will get less busy once everyone adjusts to the newly formed family or when their children and stepchildren get older. These expectations do not jibe with reality. As time goes on, many stepcouples find that their lives become filled with more activities. If you think you can wait for your schedule to lighten up before having meaningful conversations or fun with your partner, you are setting yourself up for disappointment and frustration. You may end up growing apart emotionally. To avoid this, you may have to change your priorities.

One stepmother, Ebony, complained that she felt lonely and barely saw her husband. I wanted to explore if barely seeing her husband was a feeling she had or indeed a fact. I asked her to figure out how much quality time she spent with him. He traveled a few days a week for work and coached a little league baseball team on weekends. Some days she only said good morning and good night to him, with no communication in between. There were some weeks Ebony spent less than three or four hours with him other than sleeping together. No wonder she was lonely! Her situation is not that unusual. How much quality time do you spend with your partner? For how much time do you talk to each other without the distractions of your phones and other electronic devices?

All relationships require attention to flourish. Even if you are bogged down by many responsibilities, you need to make time for your partner. Here are some ways to do so.

Connect Daily

To counterbalance the practicalities and demands of regenerated family life, it's important for partners to emotionally connect. Staying emotionally connected with your partner requires only a little effort but must be done daily, even when children are at home. There's a simple way to do this, which I learned from my friend's parents when I was in high school. As soon as they came home from work, they'd go into their bedroom, close the door, and share the events of their day and their thoughts and feelings with each other for about five to ten minutes. They did this before talking to their children, starting dinner, or doing other household activities. It was a daily ritual akin to showering and brushing their teeth. As a teenager, I was very impressed with how they prioritized their relationship, but I did not appreciate the full value of this until I was married. It really helped my husband and me stay emotionally connected with each other.

Affirm Your Love

Many couples wait for special occasions, such as birthdays or an-niversaries, to express their love for one another. This is not an effec-tive way to maintain a strong emotional connection. All of us, men in particular, need frequent reminders (by words, touch, or actions) that our partners love us. One study found that couples in which men did not receive frequent expressions of love from their partners were twice as likely to divorce or break up than those couples in which husbands did receive loving affirmations.[2] Since it doesn't take much to express your love, why not give a kiss or a compliment each day to make your partner feel valued?

Give Praise

As part of your daily conversations with your partner, don't be shy about sharing your accomplishments. A recent study found that couples reported feeling better about their relationships when acknowledged and praised by each other for a positive achievement, such as receiv-ing a promotion at work, than when supported during a crisis.[3] Your partner will be more grateful than you imagine to receive your praise for an accomplishment.

Give Hugs

Physical touch is another way to retain an emotional connection with our partners and ensure our emotional well-being. Research shows that hugs are healing.[4] They help us overcome feelings of loneliness, isolation, and anger by boosting our levels of oxytocin, also known as the cuddle hormone. Oxytocin helps us relax, calms the nervous system, and boosts positive emotions, including our sense of safety and security. Hugs also lower levels of cortisol, the hormone that effects stress, and they can lower your blood pressure, especially when you feel anxious.

Hugs can actually be more powerful than words in conveying love and understanding. They can express empathy and care and can demon-strate a commitment to your relationship. Not surprisingly, studies have shown that couples who frequently hug each other are more likely to stay together.[5] Virginia Satir, a noted family therapist, is credited for saying, "We need four hugs a day for survival. We need eight hugs a day for maintenance. We need twelve hugs a day for growth."

Schedule Date Nights

For too many stepcouples, date nights end when partners begin to live together. This is a shame, because date nights offer a much-needed break from the demands of everyday life. They are a time to have fun together, to set aside your to-do list and focus on enjoying each other's company. Date nights are essential to keeping your romantic relationship fresh and vibrant.

One stepmother, Claire, complained that her husband was unwilling to hire a babysitter for his son so they could go to the movies. He didn't want his son to be left alone or feel unimportant or jealous of their new relationship even though he spent his entire two-month summer vacation with them. Similar to this husband, many other parents see their limited time with their children as precious and will not interrupt it for any event. While this is to be respected, occasionally it is important for stepcouples to go out without children tagging along.

The truth is, it is healthy for children to see you and your partner go out alone. You are modeling how to maintain a healthy adult partnership. Plus, they will feel more secure knowing that their parent is part of a strong relationship.

Evenings (or afternoons) out don't have to be expensive. You can picnic in the park or take a walk while eating an ice cream cone. Here are a few more suggestions to make date night special:

- Make it a regular part of your lives. Schedule one each week.
- Turn off your cell phones so you are not distracted.
- Don't talk about your problems or the everyday details of your lives. Instead, talk about what interests you, discuss your plans and goals, and even share jokes with each other.
- Treat date night as a special occasion and get dressed up.

While you're at it, occasionally try a new restaurant or do something that neither you nor your partner has ever tried before. Want a scientific reason? New experiences flood the brain with dopamine and norepinephrine, neurotransmitters that help us to feel good.[6] Novel experiences help keep romance alive.

Be Flexible

If you find it difficult to make arrangements to go on a weekly date with your partner, you probably know how complicated it is to plan vacations or holidays for your regenerated family. Ex-partners are involved in this decision-making, and sometimes a lot of negotiation is required to even attend a wedding or leave town for a weekend.

Not only is patience a requirement for stepcouples, so is flexibility. Given the unique circumstances they encountered, several stepcouples with whom I worked found themselves adopting a lifestyle that they never would have previously considered before they got involved with each other. Omar, for example, had teenage children who lived in a European country. His job relocated him to the United States, where he met and married his new wife, Sharon. After a year of marriage, he felt he had to move back to Europe to help his children, who were struggling in school. It was impossible for Sharon to leave her job, so they decided to see each other twice a month. She never imagined she could be happy on her own, but she used the time to pursue hobbies and make new friends. Sharon adjusted well to this change.

Another stepcouple decided that the wife, Emma, would go on vacations with friends. Barry, her husband, had limited vacation time and wanted to spend all of it with his children. He also had less money to spend on vacations than Emma did, so he encouraged her to vacation without him. This may not have been an ideal solution, but it was one they both could live with for the time being.

Cultivate a Rich Life Outside the Relationship

There may be other activities partners in stepcouple relationships need to consider doing by themselves. Parental responsibilities may prevent one partner from going to a party or attending a lecture. Rather than stay at home because your partner can't join you, venture forth on your own. Join a book group, bowling league, or community garden project. Interesting experiences are integral to your happiness and contentment. Plus, you then bring this positive energy to your relationship.

Consider your situation: have you given up activities, such as going to the gym or hanging out with friends, because of the constraints your regenerated family has placed on your life? If you find yourself frequently feeling deprived of certain activities, then you may need to examine and change some of your choices. Make a list of activities and friendships that are important to you, prioritize them, and figure out how you can include the most important ones in your life. It's not easy to achieve a well-balanced life when you have lots of family responsibilities. It is only natural for some activities to fall by the wayside. However, you may have given up too many and need to add some back into your life. If you make yourself a priority, you won't develop resentment that life is passing you by, and your positive outlook and experiences will strengthen your relationship.

3

FINANCES

B ecause partners' financial expectations differ, money is a major source of conflict for many stepcouples. Half of the participants in my survey cited it as a big problem. Let's examine some of the reasons why this occurs.

When partners communicate openly, make decisions together, and have mutual trust and respect, the likelihood that they will manage their finances successfully, and be happier, greatly increases. Of course, that's not easy. Oftentimes past experiences cloud stepcouples' interactions. If an ex-partner took advantage of you, you may be wary of merging finances with a new one. Similarly, you may hesitate to share your financial needs and expectations with your partner, concerned he unfairly will perceive you as just as greedy or difficult about money as his ex.

Present circumstances can also bring financial complications and stress to many stepcouple relationships. Partners may differ in how they choose to spend (or not spend) their money. For example, you may resent that your partner lavishes expensive gifts on his children but doesn't ever give you any. Or maybe you did not realize that all of your partner's paycheck would go toward child support, and you are expected to make up for the shortfall. You resent being unable to spend any money on yourself or save for retirement.

Most important of all, problems develop between partners because money comes to symbolize how much we believe our partners love us. Our innermost need to feel safe and secure with our partners can be either reassured or brought into question by their spending habits. What they choose to buy may leave us wondering if they are indifferent to our needs and only concerned about their own. They may be asking the same questions of us.

THE CONSEQUENCES OF DIFFERING
FINANCIAL EXPECTATIONS

When partners don't meet the financial expectations we have of them, cracks develop in the foundation of our relationships. For example, after one stepcouple, Regina and Simon, had a baby, they decided to write wills. They were in their early thirties and had never discussed how to allocate their assets if one of them died.

When they married, Regina had moved into the apartment that Simon owned. Simon decided he wanted to leave half of his apartment to his son from a prior relationship and the other half to their new baby. Regina protested that this plan could allow her stepson to kick her out of her home if he wanted to sell the apartment. Simon's first reaction was to say that his ex-wife would never allow his son to do that. Regina was even more hurt that Simon was placing her welfare in the hands of his ex-wife and son. She understood he wanted to make sure both his children would be financially secure, but she was very upset about the precarious position he was going to place her in. She questioned how much he truly loved her. She thought about ending their relationship if he wasn't willing to protect her future as much as his children's.

Regina convinced Simon to go to an estate attorney for advice. The lawyer suggested that Simon take out three life insurance policies for his son, new baby, and Regina to protect them in case he died. He also recommended adding Regina as a co-owner to the apartment. The lawyer explained how Simon's original idea placed Regina in jeopardy. Simon finally understood the problem he was potentially creating and happily followed the lawyer's advice.

Even after their wills were drawn up and signed, Regina remained disappointed with Simon. She knew he loved her but realized he did not feel obligated to provide for her in the same way her father ensured her mother's welfare. She assumed all partners were like her father and recognized that Simon was not. He grew up believing everyone was responsible for taking care of himself or herself. She hoped Simon would change his perspective and continued to have conversations with him about how important it was to her that he considered her welfare. Most important, she learned that she had to take responsibility to protect her future well-being.

Regina and Simon were fortunate that their decision to draw up wills provided them with an opportunity to air and resolve their differences. Some of us never discuss money with our partners because we expect they will just take care of us. This can be problematic, as it was for one woman in her nineties who was dismayed to learn that her wealthy husband of 35 years had never included her in his will. When he died, she found out he had left everything to his two children from his first marriage, including the apartment they shared. After a lifetime of luxury, she was left practically penniless. Her stepchildren allowed her to continue living in the apartment, but she relied on Social Security for her monthly expenses. It pained her to remember her husband as a partner who overlooked her needs.

Some of us are afraid to talk about money because we know it will produce conflict with our partners. Olivia knew her husband expected her to include his children from his first marriage in her will. However, she didn't want them to have any of her money. To ensure this, she intended to leave a monthly stipend to her husband and give the rest to an animal shelter where she volunteered. Even though she had a 30-year relationship with her stepchildren, she had never felt that they appreciated anything she did for them. She preferred to leave her assets to a place that was meaningful to her. She hesitated to share her intentions with her husband, concerned he would be angry about her decision even though he agreed that his children didn't give her the proper respect.

While Olivia did not need her husband's permission to create her will, I encouraged her to tell him about her intentions so he could get accustomed to her plans. In the event she predeceased him, she didn't want his feelings for her marred by her will. At first he was upset with her plans, but he accepted them over time. In fact, he decided to leave a portion of his estate to the same animal shelter.

Money is a sensitive topic. By choosing not to discuss it, you may avoid conflict with your partner now but leave yourself open to future problems.

FULL FINANCIAL DISCLOSURE

Being open with your partner about your attitude and feelings about money can be cathartic and healing. Not only do you both become

aware of the reality of your financial situation, you foster trust and cooperation by sharing your financial values, attitudes, concerns, and desires.
Have you and your partner openly and honestly discussed what each of
your assets, debts, and obligations are, and how they will be handled?
Even though you may be embarrassed by the amount of credit card or
student loan debt you have accrued over the years, it is important to
disclose these facts to your partner. In most cases, honesty can lead to a
healthier, more solid relationship.

Here is a list of financial questions to help clarify your situation:

1. What are your credit scores?
2. How much money do you earn? What percentage goes toward
   child support or alimony?
3. Do you have other income? Does your family help you? Are
   you willing to accept help from parents?
4. Will your spousal support checks stop if you remarry, and have
   you told your partner this?
5. What additional child-related expenses do you pay, such as
   camp, ballet, or soccer lessons?
6. Have you read your partner's divorce decree to fully understand future financial responsibilities, such as a stepchild's college education?
7. Do you want more children? If so, are you willing to spend
   money on fertility treatment or adoption if you are unable
   to conceive?
8. Do you want your children to attend public or private school?
9. What will you do if your parents get sick? Would you be willing to contribute to their care? How much? In what way?
10. Would you help your siblings financially if they needed it? And
    would you expect them to pay you back?
11. How much money have you saved? Are you a spender or a saver?
12. Do you prefer to pay for things with cash or a credit card?
13. How do you prefer to invest savings?
14. Do you fund a retirement account? Is your ex entitled to a por-
    tion of your retirement benefits, and if so, how this will affect
    your retirement?
15. How much debt have you accrued?
16. Do you have outstanding student loans?

17. Do you want to return to school? How much money will this require?
18. Do you owe money to any family members or friends?
19. Have you ever declared bankruptcy?
20. Do you gamble?
21. Will you combine accounts and income or keep them separate?
22. Who will be in charge of paying the bills?
23. What is the maximum amount you can spend before consulting each other?

In addition to discussing the practical aspect of your finances, here are some more questions to help you better understand each other's emotions and attitudes about money:

- How did money affect your childhoods?
- What lessons have you learned about money from prior relationships?
- What are the three best purchases you've made in your life? What are the three worst?
- What is your biggest financial concern?
- What do you cherish most in life that money can buy? Are your values compatible? Can you compromise on your differences?
- What are your current financial goals?
- What are your future goals?

Don't skip or gloss over subjects that make you squirm. Even if you've chosen to live together rather than remarry just so you can avoid dealing with these sticky issues, it is still wise to talk about them. Denying, ignoring, or not dealing with these details can jeopardize your future.

HOW TO BEGIN A CONVERSATION ABOUT FINANCES

To overcome your reticence about discussing finances with your partner, take a few moments to breathe deeply and ground yourself. Visualize a positive outcome to your discussion. Be sensitive to your partner's feelings as well as your own.

The best way to start a financial discussion is by saying something like "I've been thinking about our financial situation and want us to brainstorm how we can plan for our future." This statement expresses good intentions and a desire to make joint decisions that benefit both of you.

During the conversation, stay focused on the facts, listen to each other, and try to understand each other's point of view. Do your best to not interrupt, ridicule, attack, or yell. If you don't understand or approve of your partner's ideas, ask more questions to understand his reasoning. You want to learn how to work through deadlocks and disagreements with respect, compassion, and calmness. It may take several conversations to reach a resolution that satisfies both of you. If your conversation reaches an impasse and a compromise does not seem possible, consider going to a financial advisor or counselor to help resolve your differences.

When you fully grasp the reality of your stepfamily's current and future economic situation, you can make better choices now about how to spend or save your money. Based on your conversations, you may need to write wills or revise life insurance policies.

You may want to consider a postnuptial agreement. While perceived by many as unromantic, they protect one or both partners who may bring substantial assets (or debts) to the union, or who may expect to inherit substantial assets from parents or other relatives. They also are important when one partner owns a business and wants his children to inherit the company. If you regret not having a postnuptial agreement, it's not too late. More and more stepcouples draw them up after living together or being married for a time. These documents explicitly state your preferences and keep everything open and aboveboard. Because laws change all the time, it is a good idea to consult a financial planner or lawyer for help.

SPLITTING EXPENSES

Knowing the details of your financial life can help you figure out how to split expenses. To avoid many of the arguments about money we've had in past relationships, many of us want to split expenses evenly with our partners. While fair in theory, this doesn't practically work if one of you earns considerably more money or has greater expenses, such as child support payments, medical or educational expenses, or financial responsibilities to elderly parents. You need to consider these added expenditures when determining a fair way to apportion how much each of you contributes to the household. Like couples in first unions, you can handle finances in one of three ways: (1) you can comingle all your money and maintain a joint savings and checking account from which you pay all bills, (2) you can keep your finances separate and pay your respective bills from individual savings and checking accounts, or (3) each of you can maintain separate checking and savings accounts and contribute money into a joint account from which you pay household bills. This last approach is the one most stepcouples I work with use, but there is no right or wrong method. It may take a bit of trial and error to find the best strategy for you and your partner.

I worked with one stepcouple in which the husband believed he and his new wife should comingle their resources just like he had in his prior marriage. In this case, it meant she would contribute a considerable portion of her income to pay for airline tickets so his children, who lived 3,000 miles away, could visit him every month. At first she agreed to merge incomes but quickly grew to resent that her salary was going toward this airfare. She wondered if her husband married her just so he could spend more time with his children. When I told them that most repartnered couples don't pool all of their resources, he was upset, but then he did some research and found out that this was true. He realized he wasn't being fair to his wife. They devised a budget where she would contribute equally to household expenses, but he would pay for all expenses related to his children.

Here's how one stepmother, Donna, tried to balance contributions fairly:

> *Finances were a huge issue for us when we got married. My partner would spend whatever he wanted on his daughter without consulting me, and I would end up sacrificing basic necessities. This wasn't fair to me. To fix it, I created a spreadsheet of all our monthly expenses, including gas, mortgage, and food. I kept my student loan payment and his child support payments separate and subtracted each of these from our respective salaries. Then I took the remainder of our salaries and calculated what percentage they were of our monthly income. Since I brought in 60 percent, I paid 60 percent of our*

bills, and my husband paid 40 percent. We each kept any extra money from our salaries to spend or save however we wanted. We kept our separate bank accounts and opened up a third one in which we put our portion of expenses to pay our joint bills. Plus, we both agreed to consult each other if we were going to spend more than $100, even if this expenditure was going to be paid from one of our personal accounts. We want to make decisions as a team.

This arrangement worked well for this couple. Donna overcame her resentment that her husband wasn't considering her financial needs, and her husband gained a clear understanding of how much money was in his checking account. Their tensions over money largely evaporated.

Donna has the right idea. It doesn't matter who pays the bills as long as you both are involved in making financial decisions for your family. Talking about sensitive topics and brainstorming options and alternatives will help you become a solid, secure team.

4

REDEFINE THE ROLE
OF STEPPARENT

Another crucial step in creating a happier relationship with your partner is to clarify your role as a stepparent—and to remember that there's no right way to be one. Most stepcouples don't think about, let alone discuss, their parenting expectations for each other when they first start living together as a regenerated family. Armed with good intentions, most plunge into family life without knowing what role they are expected to adopt in their stepchildren's lives. It is very common for partners to have very different expectations of what stepparents are supposed to do in the family, which can lead to conflict.

IDENTIFY STEPPARENT RESPONSIBILITIES

While some divorced parents don't expect their responsibilities to change when they begin to live with new partners, others assume their mates will lighten their load by taking on full-time maternal or paternal duties for their children. This becomes problematic when their partners expect to pitch in only occasionally. A larger, more common conflict occurs when a partner who expects full-time help with her children will not give her mate any say in the way the children are raised. Many stepparents complain they are laden with responsibility yet lack any power in the family to enforce household rules. When unspoken expectations such as these differ and are left unaddressed, it is only natural for partners to develop resentment and bitterness toward each other—and the children. To avoid these problems, it is vital for you to consider what role you want to play in raising your stepchildren and express that to your partner. You may need to have several conversations before deciding what is fair and acceptable for each of you.

If you are a stepparent, consider what responsibilities you expect to undertake for your stepchildren:

- Do you expect to take care of your stepchildren while they are in your care?
- Do you expect to teach your stepchildren the difference between right and wrong?
- Do you expect to give your stepchildren age-appropriate chores to do around your home? Do you expect to discipline them?
- Do you expect your partner to consider your opinion regarding your stepchildren's medical, academic, social, and recreational needs?

If you are a biological parent, consider what responsibilities you expect your partner to fulfill:

- Do you expect your partner to take care of your children when you are not home?
- Do you expect your partner to drive your children to activities, such as soccer practice?
- Do you expect your partner to discipline your children when they misbehave?
- Do you expect your partner to go along with the way you want to spend money on your children?

Try this exercise: Sit down with your partner and each make a list of your expectations for taking care of the children in your household. Then share the lists with each other to determine whether your expectations are aligned. Check to see if there are any obstacles out of your control that prevent you from meeting these expectations. Stepchildren, your partner's ex, and even your partner may resist your efforts. In this case, you will have to adapt your expectations to your particular situation. This will ease your frustration and maintain harmony in your regenerated family.

AVOID COMMON DIFFICULTIES

Let's examine a few common difficulties described by those who completed my survey as well as ways to avoid or lessen them.

Resistance from Stepchildren and Others

Some stepchildren resist their stepparents' involvement in their lives and particularly object when their stepparents attempt to share parenting responsibilities with their father or mother. This is one more change resulting from their parent's separation that they may find difficult to accept. For example, Nina had nine-year-old twin sons and an eight-year-old stepson whom she expected to co-parent. Luckily the boys got along well, but when they were roughhousing too much, she would give all three time-outs. Her sons accepted their punishment and moved on to other activities when it was over, but her stepson remained upset. He would then complain to his mother that Nina was mean. Nina felt trapped between a rock and a hard place. She needed to maintain order in her household but did not want to be cast as the wicked stepmother.

Nina truly loved her stepson and wanted to treat him similarly to the way she did her sons. Her sons accepted her husband's discipline without complaint. She didn't think it was fair that she didn't get the same response and respect. (By the way, Nina's experience is typical, as stepmothers tend to run into more obstacles than stepfathers.)

I explained to Nina that it is harder to build a relationship with stepchildren in spurts than when living with them full time. Nina saw her stepson every other weekend and for two- or three-week stretches each summer, while her husband interacted with her twins every day. Nina's ex-husband lived in another state, and her sons rarely saw him, so they were more accustomed to spending time with her husband than her stepson was with her. In addition, her stepson's attachment to his mother was very strong, and it was difficult for him to accept another maternal figure. By complaining about Nina's discipline, he was expressing loyalty to his mother. His mother also played a role in how Nina's stepson handled his punishment. She remained angry and resentful after the divorce, and Nina's stepson picked up and acted on these negative feelings.

I reminded Nina that her stepson was only eight years old. He was too young to describe his struggle adjusting to living in two different households, each with its own set of rules and expectations. His complaints about her punishment were an expression of his discomfort with this transition. Nina understood and felt compassion for what he was going through, and recognized she needed to change the manner in which she punished him so they could maintain a good relationship.

When Nina asked for my help, I suggested she treat her stepson more like a nephew or one of her son's good friends who was visiting them for the day. She immediately understood the difference and knew what to do. When her stepson needed a time-out, she would call her husband and let him be the primary disciplinarian for his son. Since she was able to contact him by phone during the day, she could tell him how the boys were misbehaving and how he could help her. Nina would then hand the phone to her stepson and let her husband impose the punishment. His son obeyed him and stopped complaining to his mother that Nina was treating him harshly. When she let go of her expectation to be a co-parent and placed herself in a supporting role, Nina was happier. She is not alone; most stepparents find that they have better relationships with their stepchildren when their partners take sole responsibility for disciplining their children.

When Only One Parent Is Available

Not all stepparents can step away from taking care of or disciplining their stepchildren. If their partner travels extensively for work or is deployed for active duty in the military, they have to assume full-time parenting duties. In these cases, stepcouples must maintain a united front with regard to rules children must abide by and the consequences that will be enforced if the rules are not followed.

Take this stepmother's situation:

My wife, Hannah, works full time during the day and goes to school at night. I take care of my eight-year-old stepdaughter, who lives with us full time. Before going to school yesterday, she lied to me several times. I told her that she would get punished for lying, and we would talk about it later. Hannah and I talked about what happened when she was driving from work to school, and I suggested a punishment. She countered with something else, and we came to a conclusion together. She called us during her dinner break, and we used that time to present my stepdaughter with her punishment. I did all the talking, but she knew her mother was fully aware of what she did and supported me fully. This works for us.

When a parent is absent from the home and cannot be contacted, she can announce to her children when leaving the home, "Your stepparent is in charge while I am gone. I expect you to follow the house rules. No watching TV before homework. Brush your teeth at 8:00. Go to bed at 8:30." The stepparent then enforces the house rules. If a child objects to following one of them by saying, "You're not my father (or mother)," the stepparent can calmly respond by saying, "Yes, you are right. You have a mother and a father. I'm not taking their place. Meanwhile, though, I am the adult in charge tonight, and the rule of the house is no TV until you've finished your homework. Otherwise, no TV tomorrow night!"

Maintain a United Front

If you are asking for a stepparent's help to co-parent by enforcing rules and consequences for your children, consider what rules and structure you are willing to implement. Consistency is important. When parents are strict one time, then permissive the next, it sends a message to children that parents can be swayed. Never give ultimatums unless you are prepared to carry them out—or your children won't take you seriously.

Maintaining a united front can prevent children from having too much power in their family. Some children believe they should be treated equally as adults and should have as much power to decide what restaurant to eat at or which movie to watch. While I believe children's needs must always be considered, parents are better equipped to make decisions that affect all regenerated family members. This may seem obvious, but it is quite common for divorced parents to give their children too much power, and it may take time for them to realize it is preferable and healthier to be allied with their partners rather than their children.

Here are some strategies to help you stay united:

1. Have a conversation with your partner about the preferred household rules and expectations each of you wants to maintain.

It may take several conversations to reach a consensus on which rules you will enforce.

2. Discuss who will discipline the children when discipline is needed. Ideally the biological parent will take the lead, though some stepcouples decide to share this responsibility. If you do, it is vital that your partner back you up if your stepchildren appeal your decision. If you try to discipline the kids without the solid agreement of your partner, your stepchildren will end up resenting you.

3. If you disagree with a decision the other has made, discuss it later in private. Reevaluate your rule if it's too difficult to implement.

4. Periodically hold a family meeting during which you remind your children that because you love them, it is your job as their caretakers to enforce structure and discipline. Household rules are not a form of cruelty; they teach responsibility and self-sufficiency.

Clashing Parenting Styles

Clashing parenting styles is one of the most common reasons stepcouples fight. Many of the participants in my survey complained that their partners were too lax in providing rules and regulations for their children to follow. They referred to them as Disney Moms and Disney Dads who acted more like playmates than parents to their children. Because these parents felt so guilty about potentially harming their children as a result of their divorce, they did not want to inflict further damage on them. Mistakenly, they considered structure and appropriate limits as forms of punishment, so they refused to create a set of rules for their children to follow. They also refused to give their children any chores to complete, and as a result their children were treated more like guests than household members. Their parents did everything for them, including taking their dinner plate to the sink or making their bed.

One stepmother, Cherise, diagnosed her husband with "my girls' syndrome." She thought he was overly lenient in allowing his daughters from his first marriage to watch TV all day long instead of doing their homework or cleaning their rooms. Meanwhile he insisted that his children from his current marriage do weekly chores, obey strict bedtimes, and limit the time they could play electronic games. His younger children rightfully felt the older ones were favored and became jealous of their half-siblings.

Inadvertently Cherise's husband created a divide between his children from his first marriage and those from his second by having different rules for each set of siblings. This also placed Cherise in the unpleasant situation of needing to repeatedly explain to her children that life isn't always fair, and just because their older siblings didn't have chores didn't mean they didn't have to do theirs. She also resented her husband for preventing her from asking his teenage daughters for help around the house, such as setting the table for dinner or walking the dog. Cherise's desire to treat her stepdaughters similarly to her children was squashed by her husband's guilt. Despite the fact that they held many conversations about his leniency, he refused to change the way he treated them.

Many stepcouples have conversations about providing more structure for children in the home, but when one partner lacks follow-through—even while recognizing that they are not acting in the best interest of their child—it creates frustration and rifts in their relationship. Oftentimes this situation happens in households in which both partners have children from prior relationships. It is extremely difficult to merge families when one parent has a set of rules and chores for her children to obey while the other one has none.

Cherise was forced to accept that there were two standards in her household. Her husband would not change his parenting style or give her the authority to parent her stepchildren. What can you do in this situation? Cherise gave this advice:

> *Unless your partners are neglecting or abusing your stepchildren, let them parent the way they choose to. Not your kid, not your problem. Instead, concentrate on your relationship, your interests, your career, and your own family. My relationship was saved when I stopped micromanaging the way my husband parented his children from his first marriage. Try it; it might work for you too.*

If your partner won't or can't change his or her parenting style, you too may need to abide by the acronym NMKNMP (not my kid, not my problem).

Many parents find it hard to change their parenting style despite knowing that a different method would benefit their children. If your partner is in this camp, it's important to be patient. However, if you feel you haven't made any progress in asking your partner to be more consistent, strict, or fair with her children, then you may have to change your expectations about the way your stepchildren are raised. Even though children thrive in homes where parents establish rules, structure, and expectations for appropriate behavior, you may need to accept that your stepchildren will not receive the best parenting possible—and even without it, they can still turn out to be terrific adults.

DISENGAGE WHEN NECESSARY

Backing off from making suggestions about how your partner should parent her children or giving up the parental duties you have taken over may not be an ideal solution, but it is one many stepparents are forced to accept because their partners won't or can't change. Disengaging means you decide to no longer participate in one or more activities or discussions. It does not mean that you will detach from, reject, or ignore regenerated family members. Actually, you may have a better relationship with your stepchildren if you let go of parental duties. It's far easier to establish a bond with them by doing fun activities together. Believe it or not, being a stepparent can be a joyous experience and can provide your stepchildren with fond memories that include you.

How to Back Off

Here are two examples of how some stepmothers chose to disengage. Arianna found it hard to accept that it wasn't her place to help her stepchildren. She got along very well with her two teenage stepsons and believed they were capable of doing much better in school if only they would complete their homework before playing video games or watching TV. She asked her husband to set this as a rule for them but was disappointed when he didn't enforce it. At first she would remind her stepsons to do their homework, but she grew frustrated with them when they would make excuses for doing other things first.

Arianna disliked nagging and one day had an epiphany: why should she care more about her stepchildren's education than her husband did? She realized she was fighting a no-win battle by focusing on her stepsons' study habits. They resented her for being stricter than either their mother or their father, and her husband did not like to be reminded of his lenient attitude. She realized she had to stop pestering her stepsons to complete their homework before she ruined her relationship with them. It wasn't her job to parent them; they already had two parents. She could limit her role to that of a kind adult in the household—more like a loving aunt than a third parent. This was not an easy adjustment for Arianna. At first she struggled to accept that her stepsons might not reach their potential without her help. Eventually she understood it was not her place to impose her values on them. She still shared her values with her stepsons but stopped telling them to do their homework and reprimanding them when they didn't. Letting this responsibility go eased a burden from Arianna's shoulders.

Another stepmother I worked with, Ella, shared similar concerns. She feared her stepson would not be admitted to college because of mediocre grades. She wanted him to become a confident, self-sufficient adult and believed a college education was instrumental to reaching this goal. Without being asked by her wife or stepson, she found a college preparatory class for him to attend and went as far as calling friends to see if anyone had a connection to get him into a school. She wondered why her wife and stepson did not appreciate her efforts. Then she too had a revelation: by helping her stepson now she might be doing more harm than good for him in the future. The sooner she let him stand on his own two feet, the better off he would be as an independent adult. Ella stopped intervening on her stepson's behalf but she still worried about him.

While their intentions were admirable, both of these stepmothers undertook a responsibility that was not asked of them. You too may see that your stepchild needs help. However, if your partner doesn't share your concerns, it is not your place to intervene (unless your stepchild explicitly asks for and welcomes your help). I know this seems cruel, but being a stepparent is a role similar to that of researchers in the wild observing a pride of lions: they can't intervene if one animal needs help but must allow nature to take its course.

Backing Off from Bigger Problems

"Little children, little problems. Big children, big problems." Generally this expression is true. While it's not easy to deal with small children who throw tantrums, lie, or won't go to bed, brush their teeth, or take showers, these problems are small compared to the ones teenagers can have. They may be truant from school, drink alcohol and take drugs, and steal, among other harmful activities. When stepchildren engage in any of these activities, stepparents may empathize with their struggles and yet be placed in very difficult circumstances if their partners ignore or are ineffectual in dealing with them.

Arianna's husband was not only lax about study habits, he was easygoing about everything else too. He never once punished his sons when they misbehaved. Arianna thought her stepsons would be hurt by her husband's weak parenting skills. They would never learn important life lessons, such as understanding the concept of cause and effect: one benefits from taking positive action and suffers when doing something poorly.

Arianna and her husband did agree that his sons couldn't stay in their apartment by themselves if he and she were out of town and that they would instead sleep at their mother's home. One weekend when she and her husband were visiting her family, they got a phone call from their doorman, who told them that one of her stepsons was in their apartment with seven other boys. Her husband didn't see a problem with his son holding an unsupervised party. Arianna insisted her husband call him and tell him and his friends to leave their apartment. He was hesitant to relay this message to his son.

Arianna became very frustrated with her husband. She told him she refused to be liable if one of the boys got sick in their apartment from drinking too much alcohol. She reminded him of their household rule that stipulated his sons weren't permitted to stay in the apartment for extended periods of time without an adult present. He reluctantly called his son and told him he needed to go with his friends to his mother's home. While this satisfied Arianna, she was disappointed when they returned home and her husband didn't discuss this incident with his son or punish him in any way. Without any negative consequences for disobeying the household rule, Arianna believed her stepson would not hesitate to hold another party in their apartment. With her husband's permission, she installed a camera in the apartment, notably to check on her toddler when she wasn't home but to keep an eye on the apartment as well. She wanted to know if her stepson held another party in her home when she and her husband weren't there.

Arianna made the best of a difficult situation. While her solution was not ideal, she tried to protect her interests, her home, and her safety while maintaining a good relationship with her husband and stepsons. You too may be frustrated that your partner does not discipline your stepchildren effectively. Rather than continue to try to get your partner to change his parenting style, you may need to accept the situation as it is—and find ways to tolerably live with it. Modifying this expectation is easier said than done; many stepparents struggle before they can let it go.

BE GOOD ROOMMATES TO EACH OTHER

It may not be your job to discipline your stepchildren, but you have the right to be comfortable in your home. If your stepchildren are not respecting your space, you can teach them how to be good roommates. When living under the same roof, it is fair to expect that everyone abide by certain rules. In this way, everyone in the family knows how to be considerate of each other's needs.

A stepfather, Kamal, was upset that his wife would clean up after her daughter without asking her to pick up her toys from the floor, make her bed, or take her dish to the sink after a meal. He believed that his 12-year-old stepdaughter was capable of doing these chores herself. He was particularly annoyed by his stepdaughter's poor table manners. She chewed with her mouth open and left crumbs by her placemat and on the floor by her seat. His wife never corrected her behavior.

Kamal hesitated to tell his stepdaughter to sweep up the crumbs, fearing that she would resent him if he told her to do tasks her mother wasn't willing to ask her to do. I wondered if his stepdaughter was unaware she was leaving a mess and didn't know how to clean up after herself because his wife hadn't seen the need to teach her these skills. I encouraged him to gently instruct his stepdaughter how to clean up around her plate when the meal was finished. A few weeks later, Kamal was delighted to tell me that his stepdaughter loved using a little table vacuum to clean the mess around her plate after each meal. She even cleaned the kitchen counters with it. It wasn't Kamal's place to discipline his stepdaughter, but he could ask her to be a good roommate.

The easiest way to be good roommates is to establish fair household rules that everyone will follow. To do so, you and your partner first need to have a conversation about what's important to both of you. For example, do you care if the beds are made every day? Do you care if dirty clothes are put in the hamper? How frequently do you want the toilet bowl cleaned?

Here is a list of the household rules adopted by one regenerated family:

- Keep the toilet seat down, flush after using, and close the bathroom door.
- No electronic devices at mealtimes. No phone calls during mealtimes.
- Put away toys, game pieces, and Nintendo controllers before bedtime.
- Pick up all trash (like used tissues or soda cans) on tables before bedtime.

After you and your partner come up with fair and age-appropriate household rules, include children in the conversation by telling them of the new changes. You can ask for their objections at this time. Also discuss the specific consequences if chores are not completed. You want everything to be as clear as possible to avoid confusion later on.

Belinda, a stepmother, shared her experience:

We had very frank conversations with my stepchildren that they lived in two different houses and needed to adhere to two different sets of rules. To get my stepchildren to follow our rules, I tried all the reward charts in all sorts of configurations. What truly turned out to be most effective was imposing a consequence for not completing their chores. We took away the privilege to use electronics. We also gave time limits to complete chores. We would say, "OK, you can either sweep the floor now or you can do it by one p.m. If it's not done by then, you won't be allowed to play on the Xbox for the rest of the day." I stayed calm and stuck to the point. It used to make me so mad that my teenage stepdaughters wouldn't do their laundry until I realized that if they didn't do it, they would just wear dirty clothes—which wouldn't kill them. I didn't have to do it for them. Guess what? They now do their laundry.

You can use the following strategies to encourage children to follow household rules:

- Be clear and specific about the rules. It's not fair to expect children to follow rules if they don't understand them.
- Be clear about the consequences. Just as important as knowing the rules is being aware of the consequences of breaking them. Don't expect your stepchildren to cooperate just because you explain why the rules are important. As you probably know, nagging and lecturing are a waste of your breath. Fair consequences are much more effective. Whether you use time-outs or take away a child's favorite toy, children are more apt to follow rules when something tangible is at stake for them.
- Be consistent. Once you make a rule, you must enforce it. If you don't, children won't take you or the rule seriously. You can't allow children to jump on the couch one day and then forbid this behavior the next day. Unintentionally you are giving a mixed message, and children won't know what the limits are.
- Provide positive reinforcement for the rule by saying thank you when a task has been completed.
- Ask for help. It's often easier to do a chore by yourself, but there are several benefits to asking your stepchildren for their help. You will be teaching them the value of cooperation, helping them learn new skills, and giving them a sense of accomplishment.

Parenting is the hardest job, and it is made more difficult for stepcouples who have different philosophies about the best way to raise children or for those partners who, for a variety of reasons, cannot fulfill their expected stepparenting roles. If you are in this situation, it is important that you and your partner discuss your differences and the obstacles in your path, and find compromises that will satisfy each of you. With each other's encouragement, both of you can select new household guidelines, which will benefit everyone in the family.

A Case Illustration

Many individuals experience depression and anxiety when their expectations of family life or of their intimate relationships with partners are unfulfilled. To overcome these feelings and learn how to better manage their situation, they turn to counseling for help. Let's examine the therapeutic process for one stepmother, Carly.

When Carly entered therapy, she had been married for eight years to Cody, who had one teenage girl and two young boys from a prior marriage. She was very upset that her relationship with her stepchildren had deteriorated so badly that they barely talked to her. When she first got married, everyone got along. She was especially close to her stepdaughter—they would go shopping and play tennis with each other. These activities abruptly ended when her stepdaughter asked if it was true what her mother was saying about her: that Carly was responsible for her parents' divorce. It was not at all true. In fact, Carly met her husband two years after the girl's mother left him for another man. However, after Cody's ex-wife and this man broke up, she did ask Cody if they could get back together. He refused, and married Carly.

Despite the fact that Carly had nothing to do with Cody's divorce, her stepdaughter shunned her. Instead of eating dinner with the family, she ate in her bedroom. Her behavior affected her brothers, who grew uncomfortable in Carly's presence. Carly was very upset and came to me for help.

Identify Expectations and Concerns

In our first session, I asked Carly to tell me how she envisioned her role as a stepmother. She said that since she didn't have, or plan to have, children of her own, she threw herself into the maternal role with gusto. She wanted to love and be loved by her stepchildren. She planned outings, made fun meals, and hoped to be a good influence in their lives. Since her stepchildren lived with her 50 percent of the time, she saw herself as a co-parent—an adult in the household who could politely ask her stepchildren to set the table for dinner or clean their rooms—and she expected they would listen to her.

Identify Underlying Feelings

I then asked Carly how she felt about the change in her relationship with her stepchildren. She was crushed that after years of a good relationship, her stepchildren barely tolerated her. She was afraid Cody would end their marriage because his children no longer cared for her. She wasn't happy with him either. She wanted him to explain to his children that she was not responsible for his divorce from their mother, and when he didn't, she resented the lack of support. She wanted him to get family life to go back to the easygoing way it used to be.

Identify Negative Patterns

I asked Carly to describe her reaction to the change in her stepchildren's attitude toward her. She admitted she did not handle it well. She would sulk when going out to eat with the family, which made everyone uncomfortable. To avoid feeling like an outsider in the family, Carly chose to work on weekends and encouraged Cody to take his children on vacation without her. She realized that avoiding her stepchildren was not going to heal her relationship with them.

Carly was also concerned about the number of fights she was having with Cody. She was disappointed by his lax parenting style and would yell at him for his lack of follow-through. He would remind his children to clean their rooms but never made sure they did. Cody did not like being repeatedly told he was an ineffective parent and would walk away from Carly the minute she raised her voice. This precipitated days when they did not talk to each other. After a time they would resume talking as though the fight had never occurred. They never apologized for their roles in the fight or resolved their differences. Carly realized that if she wanted a loving marriage, she and Cody had to learn how to communicate more effectively.

Reframe Expectations

Carly felt ashamed and embarrassed that her stepchildren had become emotionally distant and was uncomfortable sharing this with her friends. I explained that only 20 percent of stepchildren feel close to their stepmothers.[1] Carly was relieved to know she was not the only stepmother in this position, and she no longer had to keep it a secret.

While it wasn't necessary for her to have a close relationship with her stepchildren, I told her she had to treat them with respect and compassion. Just because they ignored her, it wasn't right for her to ignore them. She was an adult and had to act maturely by saying hello and goodbye to them. She agreed to be more considerate.

I also explained that Cody is similar to many fathers who prefer to be a fun rather than strict parent. He feels terrible that his children endured pain because of his divorce and does not want them to be hurt again. Mistakenly, he equates household rules and discipline with potential pain, so he is uncomfortable imposing any on his children. He also fears that if he tells his children how much he loves Carly, they might feel rejected and refuse to spend time with him. I added that even if Cody stepped up to the plate and did everything Carly asked of him, her stepchildren might continue to keep her at arm's length. I suggested that Carly consider accepting Cody's feelings more and recognize he was also struggling under these difficult circumstances.

Change Behavior

To defuse tension in the family, I suggested that Carly and Cody hold a family meeting during which she would apologize to her stepchildren for making them uncomfortable by sulking at dinner. I also suggested that Cody sit next to her and tell his kids that he and Carly intended to stay married forever, whether they approved or not, and that he expected them to treat her with the respect she deserved. At this meeting Carly's stepchildren should be given an opportunity to express their feelings.

Carly and Cody did hold a family meeting, which went very well, and dispelled every bit of tension with her stepsons. Her stepdaughter remained distant but would talk to Carly when Cody was present.

Carly then spoke privately with Cody and apologized for the times she lost her temper with him. She promised that in the future she would control her anger and treat him more respectfully. She added that she would share in the responsibility of planning fun activities for them to do as a couple. In the past, she had expected Cody to make all restaurant and concert reservations.

I told Carly to look for happiness and satisfaction in areas other than her family. Hobbies might prevent her from dwelling on her family's dysfunction. Following my advice, she enrolled in a calligraphy class in which she excelled so much that she started a side business doing wedding invitations. She also joined a book club and made dates to have lunch with friends. When she surrounded herself with people who enjoyed her company, Carly's self-esteem began to improve.

Carly learned to cope with painful emotions. She focused on the areas of her life she could control and no longer paid as much attention to those she couldn't.

EXPECTATION SELF-ASSESSMENT

As you are now aware, the more our expectations are aligned with reality, the more content we are. As we near the end of Step 1, consider the following question: given your particular circumstances, are your expectations realistic or do they need to be modified? To help you answer this question, consider the following ones.

Regenerated Family Expectations

- Do you expect everyone in your family to get along with each other? Do you need to revise this expectation?
- Do you expect everyone in your partner's family to welcome you into it? Do you need to revise this expectation?
- Do you expect your children and stepchildren to become friends and be open to spending time together or going on vacation together? Do you need to revise this expectation?
- If you and your partner choose to have a child together, do you expect that your stepchildren, in-laws, and other family members will support this decision and embrace this child with love? Do you need to revise this expectation?
- Do you and your partner expect to get along with each other's parents? How much time do you expect to spend with them?

- After a divorce, many grandparents pitch in to help raise their grandchildren and may expect to continue this after a new relationship is formed. Is this acceptable to you and your partner?
- How do you and your partner expect to celebrate religious holidays, if at all?
- With whom will you spend Thanksgiving and other holidays?
- Will you and your partner mutually decide where to live?

Your Expectations of Your Partner

- Do you and your partner share future goals? Where do you expect to be 10 years from now?
- What are your professional expectations? Are you ambitious? Do you expect your partner will be successful? Is it acceptable if one of you wants to stay at home rather than work outside the home?
- Do you expect to be your partner's top priority? Do you need to revise this expectation?
- Do you expect your partner will never hurt you? Do you need to revise this expectation?
- Do you expect your partner to keep all of his or her promises?
- Do you expect your partner will support your hobbies?
- Do you expect your partner to understand your needs without your telling him or her what they are?

Parenting Expectations

- Do you expect your children and stepchildren to accept your relationship with your partner? Do you need to revise this expectation?
- Do you expect your stepchildren to accept your affection and support? Do you need to revise this expectation?
- If you have children, do you expect that they and your stepchildren will be treated equally?
- Do you expect to go on vacations with just your partner or to have your children and stepchildren join you?
- Do you expect to co-parent your stepchildren or allow your partner to take on most of the responsibilities?

- How permissive or strict are you and your partner regarding child-rearing? Have you discussed how you would punish a child who misbehaves?
- Do you and your partner believe children should have age-related chores?
- Do you and your partner believe children should be given weekly allowances? How much is appropriate?
- How do you and your partner feel about financially supporting children (or stepchildren) during college and after they graduate from school? At what age do you and your partner expect your children and stepchildren to be financially independent?
- Do you expect that you and your partner will include each other's biological children in your wills?

You may need to revise some of your expectations that have not been met and that are responsible for disappointing you, frustrating you, and creating tension between you and your partner. By changing them, you can feel more satisfied with your regenerated family.

We are now ready to move to Step 2. In this section, we will focus on strengthening our emotional connection with partners by improving the ways we communicate with them.

Step 2

IMPROVE COMMUNICATION

5

THE RELEVANCE OF EMOTIONAL ATTACHMENT STYLES FOR STEPCOUPLES

No relationship is idyllic—each has its own trouble spots, rough patches, and weaknesses. The majority of stepcouples with whom I work blame specific family problems as the root of their unhappiness. Time after time I have heard "We only fight about the kids" or "We only fight about his ex-spouse." What they don't realize is that these familial troubles just fertilize their unhappiness; the root of their discontent lies in their struggle to comfortably turn to each other for emotional support.

Feelings of safety and security in a relationship are imperative for it to thrive. Luckily we can take certain steps to boost rather than damage feelings of trust during our interactions with partners, which I will outline a bit later. But first we must take a step backward and examine why feeling secure in a relationship matters and where this feeling originates. Then we need to understand the way each partner's level of security impacts the other during conflicts. Once we become aware of the extent to which insecure reactions damage our emotional connection with our partner, we can strive to become more secure by doing self-confidence-building exercises as well as modifying our reactions during conflicts to ensure our partner's feeling of security remains intact too.

Stepcouple relationships are particularly susceptible to erosion of trust. When partners try to resolve challenges, their discussions can be emotionally charged and difficult. At these times, partners can unintentionally hurt each other and weaken their emotional connection through the way they speak—or don't speak—to each other. It is all too easy to become critical, nagging, or uncooperative after reaching a frustration point when our needs are not being considered or met, when we witness our partners stand idly by when other family members disrespect us, or when we feel threatened that the problem at hand will end our relationship. Just by getting upset, by raising our voices, or by refusing to talk about a problem, inadvertently we can damage the trust partners have in us. Here's how it happens.

When feelings of distress rise during contentious discussions, many of us resort to one of two approaches to alleviate frustration and anxiety. Some of us become pushy: we demand that partners prove they care about us in their words and actions. Others withdraw from our partners because we are uncomfortable experiencing negative feelings, scared to share with partners how we've been hurt, and need to calm down and heal on our own.

Depending on the way you and your partner react during conflicts, you can increase each other's insecurities, which develop from a basic misunderstanding. You and your partner feel attacked or abandoned during conflicts by the other's pushy or avoidant reactions instead of realizing that these are attempts to alleviate emotional pain. *This misunderstanding is where the crux of the problem lies for most stepcouples.*

Most of us aren't conscious of the effect of this miscommunication. We focus all our attention during conflicts on the specific regenerated family problems we are experiencing; we don't realize we are simultaneously undermining our partners' trust in us. To make matters worse, since we aren't even aware this is happening, we don't have an opportunity to correct any false impressions and reassure partners of our love. With each harsh conversation, partners grow more wary and suspicious of each other until some believe ending the relationship is the only solution.

THE IMPORTANCE OF FEELING SAFE
AND SECURE IN RELATIONSHIPS

By the time we enter a relationship, we already have beliefs about how much we can trust our partner based on our past experiences. Some of us feel safer and more secure than others. Our individual level of security determines how emotionally close we get to our partner. The more secure we are, the more comfortable we are with intimacy; the more insecure we are, the more we prefer emotional distance. Where we stand on this continuum influences our openness or defensiveness with others. It affects how we deal with conflict—whether we try to avoid disagreements or face them without fear. It shapes the way we balance our everyday emotions—whether or not we are even-keeled or experience frequent emotional ups and downs. It even affects how we bounce back from misfortune, among other areas of our emotional life.

Those who are secure in relationships think, feel, and behave very differently than those who are insecure. Let me give you an example using a scenario experienced by most heterosexual or homosexual couples at one time or another. A husband called his wife to tell her he was leaving work and coming home for dinner. She started to cook and after 40 minutes began to wonder why he hadn't arrived home, because his commute usually took only 20 minutes. She was concerned that the meal would be overcooked and called him on his cell phone to see where he was. Her call went straight to his voice mail.

An insecure wife thinks about and handles this situation very differently than a secure one. She becomes anxious when her husband doesn't arrive home on time and assumes he was delayed by socializing with office pals or some other self-centered activity. She thinks he is being selfish and inconsiderate by delaying their meal and takes his lateness as a sign that he doesn't truly care about her. She is hurt and angry. When her husband comes home, she gives him the cold shoulder.

Truth be told, her husband was late because he was buying her a book in the basement of a bookstore. He knew how badly she wanted a specific book and was being kind and thoughtful by getting it for her. He didn't think it would take as long as it did, and since there wasn't cell service in the basement of the store, he hadn't noticed she called. When he arrived home, he was upset that she was annoyed with him, and the rest of their night was filled with tension.

Imagine the same scenario with a secure wife. She may have a fleeting concern her husband was in a car accident or caught in traffic. The thought may even cross her mind that he forgot what time they were supposed to eat dinner, but she does not assume the reason he is late is because he is putting his needs over hers. She may not like having her meal delayed but waits for his explanation before getting upset. Essentially she gives her husband the benefit of the doubt. When he comes home, she nicely asks what kept him. When she finds out he was late because he was buying her a book, she is delighted by his thoughtfulness and tells him how happy she is. He feels appreciated for being so considerate. The rest of their evening is spent in harmony.

Insecure and secure husbands will react differently when insecure wives accuse them of being inconsiderate. One type of insecure husband may be so uncomfortable with conflict that he withdraws when challenged by his wife. Inwardly he harbors a grudge for being unfairly yelled at yet avoids directly expressing his hurt feelings to his wife. Another type of insecure husband might become anxious when confronted. He will apologize for his tardiness just to maintain peace even though he doesn't believe he did anything wrong. These two ways of dealing with this situation may de-escalate tensions temporarily but sweep a larger issue—growing resentment and emotional distance—under the rug. Over time, these unaddressed feelings will cause problems for a couple. By contrast, a secure husband will react to an unfair accusation by directly and calmly telling his wife she was mistaken to assume the worst and then will reassure her of his love, as exemplified by stopping to buy her a book.

How would you react in the above scenario? How do you imagine your partner would react? Here's a confession: this really happened to me. It remains embedded in my mind because I consider myself fortunate that I restrained myself from expressing annoyance when my husband came home late one night. If I had unfairly accused him of being inconsiderate before knowing the facts, I doubt he would be interested in fulfilling any of my future desires—nor would I entirely deserve his kindness.

As you can tell from just this one scenario, the security or insecurity we feel with partners really matters. If we believe our partners are dependable and available to support us in times of need, we view them positively; consequently, peace and harmony are easier to maintain in our relationships. When we don't believe our partners truly care about us, we tend to be critical and resentful of their actions. Even if we don't communicate this judgment directly, bitterness and disappointment seep into our relationships, causing tension and problems.

EMOTIONAL ATTACHMENT STYLES

Why are some of us more secure in relationships than others? The answer, surprisingly, goes back to our infancy, when we form emotional attachment styles. These styles, which I will describe in detail below, originate in our early months of life and have an important impact on later relationships. They don't necessarily define the entire way we relate to our partners, since intervening experiences and temperament also play a huge role in forming adult attachment styles. However, the attachment patterns we establish in childhood can influence our choice of partners as well as our experiences within these relationships. They can also influence many of our beliefs about relationships, such as whether or not romantic love is enduring or temporary. Attachment styles can affect much of what happens in our relationships—how we experience jealousy, how we deal with conflict, and how easily we can forgive partners when they make mistakes, to name just a few examples. Emotional attachment styles provide a framework from which we can examine whether our emotions, thoughts, and behaviors about intimate relationships are secure and healthy or whether we need to modify them. The following is a brief history of emotional attachment theory.

An Overview of Attachment Theory

British psychoanalyst John Bowlby developed emotional attachment theory, which explains that people need emotional contact to be healthy and that these connections must also feel safe.[1] While observing infants, he noticed they shared common behaviors when separated from their parents. They actively looked for them by crying, clinging, and frantically searching the room. While other psychoanalysts at the time regarded these attempts to reunite with caregivers as signs of an infant's immature defense mechanism, Bowlby noted that these "attachment behaviors" were universal, experienced by all infants, human as well as other mammals. He theorized that crying and searching were survival mechanisms to ensure that babies stay close to the person who provides them with love, support, and care.

Bowlby also noticed infants had different reactions when their caregivers left them. His colleagues Ainsworth and Bell conducted an experiment to demonstrate these differences.[2] In their lab, they studied the reactions of year-old infants who were separated from their parents for a brief time. They found that when the parents left the room, most babies became upset and actively looked for them. When the parents returned, about 60 percent of the infants were easily comforted. They described these children as *secure* with respect to their relationship to caregivers. When some infants (about 20 percent) entered the lab with their parents, they were somewhat ill at ease. They became extremely distressed after their parents left the room. More important, they had a difficult time being soothed when their parents returned. It seemed that at the same time they want to be comforted, they also wanted to punish their parents for leaving them alone. These children were called *anxious-resistant* (or anxious-preoccupied) toward their caregivers. Ainsworth and Bell observed a third pattern of attachment in infants that they called *avoidant*.[3] These avoidant children (about 20 percent) did not appear too distressed when their parents left the room. Upon their parents' return, they actively avoided contact with them by turning their attention to the toys on the laboratory floor.

A note of clarification: the usage of the words "secure" and "insecure" is limited to describe differences in the kinds of relationships infants develop with their primary caregivers. They are not intended to label or categorize infants' personalities as secure or insecure.

After Ainsworth and Bell's study, other researchers identified a fourth attachment category called *disorganized attachment*.[4] Compared to anxious and avoidant infants, who behave consistently when separated from and reunited with their caregivers, disorganized infants don't have the same reaction each time their caregivers leave and then return; their behavior lacks a coherent structure. Sometimes they cry, while other times they look dazed and confused. When their caregivers return, they can demonstrate ambivalent behavior by first running up to their caregivers and then immediately running away. Initially these children seek comfort, but as they approach their caregivers, they become fearful. These approach/avoidance behaviors can result from being hurt or traumatized by the people who also provide them with safety and security.

Secure attachments are formed when both the primary caregiver and the infant can sense each other's feelings and emotions. Infants seek comfort from their caregivers when they are tired, hungry, ill, or in pain, or when something in the environment, such as a loud noise, scares them. When caregivers can respond to and soothe them, these infants form a secure attachment bond. This provides them with a foundation from which they can develop meaningful connections with others, explore the world with curiosity, and balance their emotions in the future.

It can be harder for some infants to form stable relationships, be open to new experiences, and regulate their emotions as adults when their caregivers don't respond consistently to them, or reject or ignore them when they are distressed. Some caregivers are unavailable, unaware, or unable to comfort their babies. They may not be present when an infant needs them, they may not know how to soothe infants, or they may be too self-absorbed to notice an infant's cry of distress. Those caregivers who consistently reject or ignore their infants' needs tend to produce children who tend to avoid contact with others. The ones who react inconsistently to infants, or who interfere with their activities, tend to produce infants who explore less, cry more, and are more anxious.

Please note that attachment theory is not suggesting that some parents do not love their babies as much as other parents. However, some are more attuned to their babies' needs and better able to comfort them than other parents. Babies' temperaments also are a factor in how easily they can be soothed.

Using Attachment to Understand Your Relationship

Professors Cindy Hazan and Phillip Shaver wondered if the emotional attachment styles that developed in infancy extended to romantic relationships, since both types of relationships share certain features.[5] For example, infants and their caregivers as well as romantic partners feel safe when the other one is nearby and responsive, and insecure when the other is inaccessible. Both sets engage in intimate physical contact, and both share discoveries with one another. To test their hypothesis, Hazan and Shaver asked subjects in their revised questionnaire (see below) to select one of the sentences to best describe how they felt in a romantic relationship.[6] (Note: The terms "close" and "intimate" refer to psychological or emotional closeness, not necessarily to sexual intimacy.)

   _____ A. I am somewhat uncomfortable being close to others; I find it difficult to trust them completely and difficult to allow myself to depend on them. I am nervous when anyone gets too close, and often others want me to be more intimate than I feel comfortable being.

_____ B. I find it relatively easy to get close to others and am comfortable depending on them and having them depend on me. I don't worry about abandonment or about someone getting too close to me.

_____ C. I find that others are reluctant to get as close as I would like. I often worry that my partner doesn't really love me or won't want to stay with me. I want to get very close to my partner, and this sometimes scares people away.

Statement A indicates an avoidant style, statement B represents a secure style, and statement C indicates an ambivalent/anxious style.

Does one of these sentences describe you more than the other two? Which sentence best describes your partner? If you are unsure, here is another way to assess your predominant style. Ask yourself what happens when you experience conflict:

- Do you stay calm? (secure)
- Do you try to stop the argument by running away, crying, not sharing your true feelings, feeling afraid, or wanting to hide? (avoidant)
- Do you raise your voice, shout insults, or call your partner names during conflicts? Can you be demanding, controlling, critical, sarcastic, aggressive, or threatening at these times? (anxious)

Interestingly, Hazan and Shaver found results similar to Ainsworth and Bell's.[7] About 60 percent of their study sample were secure in their relationships, while the remaining 40 percent were evenly divided between anxious and avoidant (including disorganized) styles. This one study spawned an entire new field of psychological inquiry. In the past 30 years, hundreds if not thousands of research projects have expanded and refined our knowledge of emotional attachment theory. Research subsequent to Hazan and Shaver's distinguishes two types of avoidant styles in adults (dismissive and fearful), which correspond to the single avoidant attachment style in children.

Researchers began to realize that individuals do not neatly fit into one category of attachment style or another, so many revised their view of individual differences and currently conceptualize and measure attachment style differences by degree. That is to say each of us has aspects of secure, avoidant, and anxious attachment styles, with some of us leaning toward one style more than another. It is not important for you to know where you and your partner specifically fall on each scale, but you do need to identify your most frequent reaction to conflict with your partner.

Professors Mario Mikulincer and Phillip Shaver conceptualized that there are two attachment style dimensions, an anxious one and an avoidant one.[8] Where people lie on the anxiety dimension indicates the degree to which they worry whether a partner will be available and responsive in times of need. Those who score high on this dimension tend to worry that their partners will be unavailable or inattentive to their needs, while those scoring on the low end perceive their partners as responsive. A person's position on the avoidant dimension indicates the extent to which he or she distrusts a partner's good intentions and strives to maintain independence and emotional distance. People who score on the high end of this dimension prefer to be self-reliant and maintain an emotional distance from others. They do not want to rely on partners or be relied upon, while those who score on the low end are more comfortable with intimacy and interdependency. These two scales reflect a person's sense of attachment security as well as his response to threats and distress.

It is possible to score on the high or low end of either attachment dimension or somewhere in the middle of each continuum. Those who score low on both scales are secure and tend to react calmly during conflicts with partners. Those who score high on the anxious scale and low on the avoidant one desire closeness and intimacy with partners but fear rejection and abandonment. When they feel threatened in a relationship, they have difficulty controlling their emotions and look to partners for reassurance. At these times they tend to become clingy and demanding, using "hyperactivating" strategies to cope.[9] Those who score high on the avoidant dimension and low on the anxious one tend to ignore or repress their emotions when they experience a relationship threat. They prefer to deny their feelings and use "deactivating" strategies to cope. Finally, people who score high on both the anxious and avoidant scales tend to fall within the fearful-avoidant group. They desire and fear closeness and use both hyperactivating and deactivating strategies to cope.

Our position on these two scales can change depending upon several factors. We can react more securely to conflict when involved with a secure partner or develop more insecure reactions when a partner is avoidant or anxious, which is why it's less important to know exactly where you and your partner lie on these scales than it is to identify the strategies you use during conflicts with each other. By understanding those reactions, we can begin to develop healthier ways to communicate with our partners to create and sustain a satisfying, loving relationship.

6

UNDERSTAND EACH ATTACHMENT STYLE AND ITS UNIQUE COPING REACTION

Many of our reactions to partners during conflicts stem from emotional attachment styles we developed in childhood. Do we remain calm during conflicts with partners, do we get very upset, or do we withdraw from them? Can we forgive partners when they have hurt us? Do we feel compassionate toward partners during conflicts? Our emotional reactions affect many aspects of our lives, including our self-confidence and the well-being of our relationships.

TYPES OF REACTIONS

Let's examine in more depth the characteristics of each style to give you a framework from which you can better understand why you and your partner feel, think, and behave the way you do, particularly during conflicts with each other. Before we get started, please note that throughout the remainder of the book I provide examples of communication patterns used by secure and insecure partners. For the sake of simplicity, I refer to them as secure, anxious, or avoidant partners. These adjectives specifically describe one's reaction to conflict with a partner (and possibly with others, such as family members, friends, and colleagues) and are not meant as an overall or broad classification of one's personality. For instance, a partner can be anxious in a relationship but confident in her career. Similarly, it is possible for a partner to avoid conflict in his relationship yet assertively pursue hobbies and other interests.

Secure Reactions

Those who are secure in their relationships tend to be confident and believe they are worthy of love and care. They are comfortable with both intimacy and independence and seek to balance these in their relationships. They trust that their partners are dependable and will comfort them in times of need. They don't worry about abandonment. They trust that their relationship is strong and can resist any challenges. They can tolerate some emotional distance from partners; however, when they begin to feel too isolated from them, they initiate contact.

Securely attached individuals can calmly and clearly ask their partners for the emotional support they need, whether it is to brainstorm about a problem or be comforted by a hug. In addition, they empathize with their partners during their times of struggle and provide help. They accept partners despite their faults. During times of distress, secure individuals can regulate their emotions. When threatened by a partner's negative behavior, they can express anger in a controlled manner, without extreme hatred or hostility. They try to resolve conflicts constructively.

There are many advantages to feeling secure in an intimate relationship. Not only do our relationships lack unnecessary drama, our minds and bodies can relax because we don't feel threatened in any way. We have more time and energy to have fun with others or to enjoy the activities we like. We are also more open to trying new experiences, making life richer and more interesting.

However, there is one drawback: securely attached people may not pick up on potential threats, insults, or bad treatment as quickly as those who are avoidant and anxious and, therefore, react more slowly to them. For example, Roger and his sister Aileen both got new bosses. Roger is more secure than Aileen and did not realize his new boss wanted to replace him until it was too late for him to react. He was forced to accept a buyout from his company and retire early. On the other hand, his sister, who tends to be anxious in all relationships and thus very sensitive to verbal and nonverbal cues, knew from the moment she was introduced to her new manager that this woman wanted to replace her and got a jump start on her job search. People with anxious attachment styles notice the slightest shifts in attitudes and behaviors, and while they may misinterpret these nuances as rejection when they are not, they do benefit from their heightened sensitivities during real threats.

In summary, secure partners

- are comfortable with intimacy and express love easily,
- feel valued and loved by their partners,
- feel confident that their partners will support them in times of need,
- seek intimacy and closeness from partners when upset,
- are comfortable with commitment,
- are reliable and consistent,
- communicate relationship issues well,
- are able to compromise during arguments,
- recover from fights with partners without lingering negative emotions,
- are able to make mutual decisions with partners, and
- are straightforward and direct in dealing with partners.

Avoidant Reactions

Those who score on the high end of the avoidant dimension generally value their independence and prefer to take care of themselves rather than depend upon others for emotional support. Their childhood experiences have often led them to believe they can't trust that others will be available to help during stressful times, so they strive to be as self-reliant as possible and expect partners to be equally self-sufficient. Because of this belief, they can resent partners who ask for help and get angry with them if they feel they are being pushed into doing a favor for them against their will. They have trouble supporting others during stressful times. Instead of feeling compassion for partners in distress, they often feel pity and disdain.

Those with avoidant tendencies have difficulty sharing feelings, thoughts, and emotions with partners. As a result of bottling up their emotions, they often feel lonely in relationships. They tend to make excuses, such as needing to work long hours, to avoid intimacy. In addition, they have tendencies to take partners for granted, believing they would be just fine without a relationship.

Avoidant individuals desire peace at any price and will do their utmost to avoid conflict despite any negative consequences. To avoid arguments, they will let partners make most decisions, which often leads to unsatisfactory outcomes. Their partners end up choosing their own preference, since they don't know what their avoidant partners desire. Avoidant partners then resent them for not satisfying their needs. Despite this, they remain too uncomfortable to clearly communicate their needs and desires to partners.

During conflicts with partners, avoidant types may look calm, but they are actually scared and will do their utmost to avoid, ignore, or resist intimate and emotional conversations, behaviors referred to as "deactivating strategies."[1] They prefer to keep their emotions separate from their thoughts and actions and deal with problems by using logic to explain their position. This can frustrate and anger partners who experience avoidant partners as defensive and insensitive. The avoidant partners will then feel bad that they cannot solve the problem, so they will withdraw to a private space to soothe feelings of inadequacy or to ruminate about what has occurred. Many of their partners then feel abandoned.

Avoidant individuals do not like to experience strong, negative emotions, such as anger or fear, and try to repress them during conflicts. Because they haven't expressed these feelings at the time of the conflict, the anger can emerge later. They can hold grudges for a long time, harboring strong feelings of revenge for having been hurt, and have trouble forgiving partners.

This type of avoidant behavior is not always restricted to partners. Here's an example of marital problems one man experienced because he avoided a much-needed conversation with his son. After Kevin's divorce, he dedicated himself to spending all his time with his son, Mathew, a quiet and socially awkward child. He did not socialize with friends or other family members when they were together. He didn't even go out on any dates. A few years went by before Kevin met Julia at a conference and asked her to join him for dinner. They dated for several months before Kevin introduced her to Matt, then 11 years old. A year later, Kevin and Julia got married. Matt was indifferent to her. He wouldn't look at her, talk to her, or play games with her. Kevin hoped that in time his son would grow to love and cherish Julia. He was too uncomfortable to ask Matt to make an effort to interact more with Julia, fearful that after this conversation, his son would no longer want to spend time with him. His discomfort created many fights with Julia, who was disappointed that Kevin did nothing to encourage Matt to relate with her. Most of their marital struggles could have been avoided if Kevin had been willing to talk honestly to his son.

In summary, partners with avoidant tendencies

- value independence greatly,
- have an inflated view of their ability to be self-reliant,
- devalue partners,
- don't trust that partners are dependable to provide support,
- withdraw from partners when stressed,
- fear partners will take advantage of them,
- emphasize boundaries in relationships,
- have difficulty sharing feelings with partners,
- send mixed messages to partners, and
- feel the need to escape during disagreements or will "explode" in anger.

Anxious Reactions

Those who are anxious in relationships highly value intimacy and want to spend as much time with partners as possible. They don't believe they can survive emotionally on their own and look to partners to help them feel complete. When conflicts arise in their relationships, they become frightened that their partners don't share the same level of commitment and will eventually leave them. Their fears can precipitate physical symptoms: they may experience a racing heart, break out into a sweat, or have stomachaches and headaches.

To reduce their fear of rejection and abandonment, anxious types use "hyperactivating" strategies to cope: they become clingy, demanding, and possessive of partners.[2] They may try to control partners' actions and social interactions—going as far as governing what hobbies partners should pursue, whom they should talk to, or how they should spend money. This can often drive away partners, which reinforces an anxious person's fear of impending abandonment.

When a relationship fear is triggered, anxious types seek reassurance from their partners that they are loved. They find themselves texting, calling, or emailing partners repeatedly until they get a response. It is hard for them to think about or do anything else when in this state.

Ironically, when partners do tell them how much they love them, anxious types don't necessarily trust, or feel comforted by, this reassurance. The intensity of their anxiety is so overwhelming that nothing quells their fears. And repeatedly asking for reassurance triggers more anxiety because they fear they are pushing partners away by being too needy and demanding. Their fears can escalate until they lash out in anger at partners. They then are filled with remorse and despair that they have irreparably destroyed their relationship. They believe their situation is hopeless and become very depressed. It is very hard for them to return to a state of calmness.

Those who have anxious attachment styles tend to suffer from low self-esteem and don't trust that partners accept and love them for who they are. They believe they must please their partners (as well as family members and friends) to avoid being abandoned. Therefore, they bend over backward to accommodate their partners' needs, even if doing so jeopardizes their own welfare and happiness. They end up physically and emotionally exhausted and resent their partners for the efforts they expended on their behalf.

Let's take another look at Kevin's family. Julia, Kevin's wife, was an anxious type who believed that her stepson, Matt, had the power to destroy her marriage. She didn't think he liked her or approved of her marriage to his father, and she worried he might complain to his father about his unhappiness. She knew how much Kevin loved Matt and believed if Kevin were forced to choose one over the other, he would choose his son. Whenever she thought about this, Julia experienced stomachaches, had trouble sleeping, and struggled to focus at work. When she discussed her apprehensions with Kevin, he dismissed them as ridiculous and ended the conversation (remember that he has avoidant reactions). His withdrawal hurt Julia. She thought he was being insensitive and disinterested in her needs and felt even more insecure. She was so distressed that she had trouble feeling any compassion for the discomfort Kevin may have been experiencing.

In summary, partners with anxious tendencies

- desire closeness in relationships and are unhappy when not in a relationship,
- worry about rejection and are hypervigilant about monitoring their partner's commitment level,

- are preoccupied about their relationship,
- fear that small acts will ruin the relationship and believe they must work hard to keep their partner's interest,
- are suspicious that their partner will be unfaithful,
- have low self-esteem and doubt their ability to handle life's challenges without help, and
- feel unworthy and inadequate when their partner doesn't show reciprocal commitment to the relationship.

THE SIMILARITIES BETWEEN AVOIDANT AND ANXIOUS ATTACHMENT STYLES

Partners with anxious and avoidant tendencies seem to have very different characteristics. To give just a few examples, anxious individuals experience emotions intensely, while avoidant ones seem cool and collected, almost devoid of emotions. Those who have an anxious attachment style are more likely to get jealous, reveal personal information, and commit to a relationship than those with avoidant styles. However, they share one major characteristic: an underlying feeling of insecurity that makes it impossible for them to trust or rely on their partners for support. They are both very sensitive to being abandoned and are quick to assume that a small difference in their partner's behavior, such as cutting a phone conversation short or being quiet during dinner, indicates that rejection is not far off. But those who tend toward either style can learn to adapt in ways that will establish healthy and happy relationships.

7

THE CLASH OF EMOTIONAL ATTACHMENT STYLES

Conflicts between couples are perfectly normal. It's not possible or necessary for partners to agree about everything. It's how couples deal with their differences that is paramount to the success or failure of their relationships. Are their reactions secure or insecure? Do partners treat their differences with respect? Do they listen to and acknowledge each other's point of view, or do they quickly become critical and defensive and try to end the conversation as quickly as possible? Are partners willing to negotiate and compromise with each other, or are they unwilling to budge from their respective positions? And once conflicts are over, do partners feel their relationship is on solid footing, or are they left with a sinking feeling that they can't depend upon each other to be trustworthy teammates? The answers to these questions indicate the difference between a healthy, loving relationship and a fragile one, and in large part can be attributed to the security level of each partner.

Based on each partner's attachment style, we can predict with fairly decent accuracy how couples will communicate during conflicts. Let's examine the various combinations.

SECURE + SECURE

If both partners are secure, they deal with disagreements calmly and openly. Trust, empathy, and openness are already present in their relationship, so when they differ, they can listen to and acknowledge each other's feelings without criticism, contempt, or defensiveness. They are kind and compassionate with each other. Relationships are generally healthy when both partners are secure.

When partners are secure with each other, they look to each other for support during stressful times. This is more helpful than you might imagine, as evidenced by scientific research. In one study, research participants were placed in an MRI machine and held a stranger's hand.[1] When they were told their feet were going to be shocked, their brain waves went haywire. They reacted very differently when holding their partner's hand. Their brains did not respond nearly as strongly to the threat of shock, and they experienced the shock much less painfully than those who held the hand of a stranger.

There are other benefits to a supportive relationship. Partners are more likely to take better care of themselves by exercising regularly and eating nutritiously. Their self-esteem increases when secure partners support their goals and encourage them to pursue new activities and opportunities.[2] Plus, they cope more easily with challenges when involved with a trustworthy partner. Their level of cortisol, the stress hormone, does not rise as sharply as in those individuals whose partners are anxious or avoidant.[3,4]

It's not always possible for both partners in a relationship to be securely attached. But even if only one partner is secure, it can go a long way to stabilize a relationship. Secure partners can reassure anxious ones of their love and can tolerate the withdrawal of an avoidant one during stressful times.

AVOIDANT + AVOIDANT

Problems in relationships are most likely to develop when both partners have propensities toward either anxiousness or avoidance. When both partners have avoidant reactions, they sweep problems under the rug and refuse to discuss them. Although they may stay together for a long time, they may grow emotionally distant from each other and eventually split up.

ANXIOUS + ANXIOUS

By contrast, when both partners share anxious tendencies, they can have a stormy relationship. You might think they can relate to each other's need to be reassured, but they lose patience with each other when their attempts to soothe each other's anxiety fail. Doubt then creeps in about how secure the relationship is, and this insecurity leads to emotional disconnection from each other.

AVOIDANT + ANXIOUS

It is actually quite common for avoidant and anxious types, just like Kevin and Julia, the couple discussed earlier, to end up in relationships. Avoidant individuals are adept at maintaining an emotional distance from others, and while secure people tend to accept their rejection and move on, anxious types are willing to put in the extra effort to get them to open up. However, relationships between partners with avoidant and anxious styles often have more problems, since they are prone to misunderstand and hurt each other when they disagree. This combination of stepcouple partners is the most prevalent one that I have worked with in my psychotherapy practice and will be the main focus of our discussion of "the stepcouple shuffle" in the following chapters. Typically individuals who are avoidant are threatened by their anxious partners' emotional volatility and outbursts during conflict and want to get as far away from them as possible. This frustrates anxious types who believe if they don't immediately resolve a problem, their relationship will be in jeopardy. So they continue to seek a resolution to the conflict, while the avoidant ones try even harder to escape. Hurt feelings and mistrust arise from the push/pull battle of these emotional attachment styles.

Can you relate to the following typical conflict between anxious- and avoidant-type partners? Despite doing her best to establish a loving relationship with her stepson, Matt, Julia didn't feel she made any headway. He ignored her or gave one-word responses to her questions. For example, during dinner, Julia would ask Matt questions about his day. What did he do at school? Did he have fun at soccer? Matt would respond to her with a grunt. Kevin never encouraged his son to share more information with Julia. She interpreted her husband's passivity as an example of his lack of support for her in developing a relationship with his son.

There were other occasions during which Kevin's son totally ignored her. Julia would come home after work when Kevin and Matt were playing a board game or watching TV. Kevin would say hello, but Matt didn't greet her. Julia felt very hurt and disrespected when he didn't acknowledge her presence. Again, Kevin never told Matt to say hello to Julia, which she took as further proof that Kevin didn't care if his son was rude to her.

One night in particular haunted Julia. At dinner, Matt talked about soccer practice and how his teammates weren't playing cohesively. Kevin said, "You know I'm on your team." Julia felt excluded and hurt by this comment. By using the pronoun "I," Kevin implied Julia wasn't on his son's team. For Kevin this was a throwaway comment he immediately forgot, but Julia remembered it for a long time. In her mind it symbolized a coalition Kevin was forming with Matt against her, something she called "betrayal bonding." Rather than encouraging his son to form a relationship with her, Julia believed Kevin actually prevented it by being possessive of Matt's time and attention. He was strengthening his bond with his son by keeping her out of their inner circle. This disappointed Julia, and she saw it as one more example of Kevin's need to put a close relationship with Matt ahead of their relationship.

Following these incidents, Julia did what many of us do to make sense of a crazy and overwhelming world: make assumptions. All of us tend to do this whether we are secure, avoidant, or anxious; our emotional styles influence the meaning we ascribe to the circumstance. Based on Julia's anxious attachment style, she built a case that she could not count on Kevin to stand by her side and to support her when she was most vulnerable and needed help.

When Julia was an infant, her mother was inconsistently available to meet her emotional needs. Sometimes her mother was very attentive, and other times she was cold and indifferent. At a young age, Julia developed a fear of abandonment. To prevent it, she became clingy to make sure her mother was by her side. As a grownup, Julia did not latch on to Kevin's knee, but she demanded his time and attention. When any conflict arose in their relationship, she became anxious that Kevin was going to leave her, sought his reassurance, and pestered him until she was convinced he indeed did love her.

Julia and Kevin fought when her anxieties were triggered, such as the time when Kevin passively stood by when Matt did not greet her. After this, she tried to get him to understand how his son hurt her feelings. Kevin, however, wasn't able to soothe her by acknowledging her emotional pain because of his experiences as an infant. His mother was overly protective and vigilantly watched everything he did. He felt he was always on a very short leash. To prevent feeling smothered by his mother, he sought privacy. This need for breathing room continued into his adulthood. When he felt anything was demanded of him emotionally, he quickly felt overwhelmed and wanted to run away and be left alone. When Julia expressed hurt feelings, Kevin felt pressured and did what he could to end the conversation as quickly as possible.

During their disagreement, both Julia and Kevin reverted to their childhood ways of handling distress. Julia turned to Kevin to quell her insecurities about their relationship. Rather than hear her request as a plea for reassurance, Kevin heard it as a declaration of disappointment that he wasn't pleasing her and that she was going to leave him. The thought of rejection overwhelmed him, and to stop this fear, he withdrew from Julia. Julia and Kevin didn't mean to scare each other, but her pushiness and his withdrawal triggered each of their childhood attachment issues.

When we are upset, we don't always take the most direct route to get what we want from our partners. Oftentimes we don't even know what we are seeking. While Julia did want Kevin to encourage his son to form a relationship with her, mostly she wanted Kevin to acknowledge and validate her feelings and reassure her that it didn't matter how Matt felt about her. She wanted Kevin to tell her he loved her and their relationship was solid.

Kevin didn't realize this was what Julia wanted. He took her complaint literally and responded accordingly. He said that Matt was quiet and withdrawn from everyone he interacted with, not just Julia. While this was true, it did not reassure her. She again tried to get Kevin to acknowledge how hurt she was when her stepson ignored her. She gave him specific examples of the times this happened, hoping to trigger a sympathetic response. Instead Kevin became defensive and said Matt was just being a kid, and that this was how kids behaved toward adults.

Kevin's response escalated Julia's distress, and she began to worry that Kevin was not as committed to their relationship as she was. She believed he was criticizing and blaming her for not having a warmer relationship with her stepson. She felt the need to defend herself and then redirected the blame to Kevin. She raised her voice and criticized him for not backing her up when Matt did not respond to her questions. This remark really upset Kevin, who now felt that Julia was criticizing his parenting abilities. He reacted by attacking her and then retreating. As Julia became more heated, Kevin withdrew more into his shell until he stopped the conversation by going into the den to watch a football game. Julia felt Kevin was selfish, uncaring, and distant, while he thought she was nagging, critical, and controlling. They both walked away from the conversation feeling misunderstood and insecure.

By many stepcouples' standards, Julia and Kevin's conversation was not particularly harsh or confrontational, yet their disagreement planted seeds of doubt about the stability of their relationship. Embedded within this conversation were questions about whether they could trust each other to be totally committed to their relationship. Could they turn to each other for support when upset? Would their love be fractured by their differences?

When one partner begins to doubt the other's reliability and availability to provide emotional support, the relationship falters. After their disagreement, Julia wondered but did not directly ask Kevin where his loyalties lay. She wondered if he was on her team, or if he would stand by passively and allow his son to ignore her. She questioned whether she should emotionally open herself up to him in the future. She didn't trust that Kevin would react sensitively to her when she was most vulnerable. And Kevin worried that if Julia grew unhappier, she would leave him. He wondered if she thought she would be better off with another partner. Neither partner expressed their feelings to the other—instead they each inferred what they thought the other was feeling from their words and actions. Kevin never said he favored his son over Julia, and Julia never said she would leave Kevin. And yet they ended up feeling increasingly anxious and avoidant.

Can you relate to this conflict? Have you and your partner inadvertently scared or hurt each other during conflicts because of your different attachment styles? Even if you and your partner don't raise your voices or call each other names during a disagreement, you still may be sending the message that you don't have each other's backs and cannot be relied on in times of need. Inadvertently, you may have opened each other's childhood wounds and damaged your emotional connection with each other. The next chapters will teach you how to break out of this negative pattern and create an open, loving, and caring way to communicate in which your emotional needs can be met.

8

THE STEPCOUPLE SHUFFLE

Over time, many stepcouples develop harmful communication patterns during conflicts that damage their trust in each other. The most common of these patterns is one that I call the *stepcouple shuffle*. It has just two steps that are repeated over and over again during a fight: (1) An anxious partner who wants to resolve a problem or is irritated by something approaches his partner to seek his help. (2) In anticipation that this discussion will involve conflict and hoping to avoid it if at all possible, the avoidant counterpart distances himself by taking a step back. That's the extent of the stepcouple shuffle: one step forward by anxious partners, one step back by avoidant ones. (During fights, secure partners don't take approach or avoidant steps; they stand still.)

Sometimes avoidant partners take the first step in the stepcouple shuffle. Unable to ask for help or comfort from their partners, they withdraw to a private spot or disengage from a conversation to soothe distressed feelings. Anxious counterparts often misinterpret this backward step as rejection. Confused and upset by the sudden withdrawal, they pursue their partners, seeking clarification that they haven't done anything to harm the relationship. Avoidant partners don't realize anxious partners are merely seeking reassurance; they experience the pursuit as an attack and retreat even farther.

Regardless of who takes the first step, once it is taken, the stepcouple shuffle takes a predictable, tension-filled path. Anxious partners grow increasingly frustrated and angry that they aren't getting the cooperation and assistance they want from avoidant partners, so they raise their voices and become critical in the hope it will get their partners to respond. Avoidant partners defend themselves and then seek solitude to soothe their fear that the relationship is in jeopardy. These conversations can last for a short or long time, but the outcome is certain: the topic of conversation is left unresolved, and partners grow more isolated and disconnected from each other.

UNDERSTAND THE DESTRUCTIVE POWER OF THE STEPCOUPLE SHUFFLE

Consider Kevin and Julia, described earlier, as an example of a couple whose marriage was jeopardized by the stepcouple shuffle. You wouldn't imagine their relationship would be in trouble just because Julia wanted a closer relationship with her stepson, Matt. Neither she nor Kevin lied to each other or breached the relationship in a way we typically identify as threatening to a marriage, like having an affair. Yet major betrayals aren't required to damage trust.

Julia and Kevin believed their problems stemmed from their differing perspectives about parenting. If only they could find a compromise on effectively parenting Matt, all their problems would be resolved. They believed they fought because they didn't express themselves clearly and were misunderstood by the other. So after a disagreement, they tried to make up by clarifying their comments to restore emotional harmony. Unfortunately, this method never worked, since it wasn't the content of the conversation that led to their emotional disconnection from each other.

I explained to Julia and Kevin the principles of emotional attachment theory and assured them that even though anxious and avoidant reactions differ greatly, those with different styles share a desire to restore a feeling of safety with each other. If couples understood the underlying meaning of each other's anxious and avoidant reactions during conflicts, they would see the common desire to feel secure with each other and better navigate the path to communicate what they are really feeling.

At first Julia and Kevin balked when I told them it was the clash of their emotional styles during conflicts that was harming their relationship more than just their parenting differences. Julia had more trouble believing this. She kept referring to times Kevin did not ask Matt to say hello to her. If only he had insisted his son respect her, their relationship would be great. I acknowledged that it would help if Kevin helped

Matt develop better social skills, but it wouldn't be enough to heal their relationship. I asked her how she felt during conflicts when Kevin didn't acknowledge her feelings and withdrew from her. She admitted she felt rejected and questioned whether Kevin truly loved her.

It was not only Kevin who scared Julia by refusing to change his relaxed parenting style, a threat she perceived could end their marriage. Julia's behavior also scared Kevin, as I explained to her. She reacted with anger when Kevin stonewalled her and would end up making critical and mean comments to him. For instance, she once called him a wimp and a coward. Although Julia was a kind and gentle person, when she got angry, her voice was strong and powerful. And once she got going on a rant, it was difficult for Kevin to intervene. (Not that he tried very hard.) Even though she apologized afterward, her words still hurt. He didn't think she respected him, and he feared their relationship would fail because he couldn't make her happy.

Julia was shocked and upset when Kevin admitted that he grew scared during their fights and that his insecurity lingered long after the fights were over. She agreed she had a temper and would make hurtful comments to Kevin that she later regretted. She just wanted him to change his parenting style so their marriage would be secure; she never meant to scare him. Up until now, she had seen herself as loving and kind. In fact, she felt powerless in her marriage and saw herself as a victim who suffered as a result of Kevin's ineffective parenting. She believed he had all the control and that he was the only one who could eliminate the one issue that caused their conflict.

It was a major revelation for Julia to realize how much she hurt Kevin during fights and how her comments slowly destroyed his positive feelings for her. Her responses diminished her chances of Kevin's listening to her and may have made him less willing to change his parenting style. She now understood that her behavior was partly responsible for increasing her insecurities and for exacerbating the problems in her marriage. Kevin also realized that the more he withdrew into his shell, the more upset Julia became, and the more he experienced her wrath. If he was willing to deal with problems immediately, she wouldn't get as angry with him, and he wouldn't be as scared their relationship was headed for divorce.

RECOGNIZE THE IMPACT OF
THE STEPCOUPLE SHUFFLE

Recognizing the negative impact of the stepcouple shuffle was significant for both Kevin and Julia. They asked how they could improve their relationship and strengthen their bond with each other. I explained that once they realized their anxious and avoidant reactions actually are a desire to reconnect with, rather than separate from, each other, their perception of each other would change. They wouldn't ascribe such bad motives to the other and would then be more likely to respond to each other in a compassionate and soothing way that would strengthen their relationship.

This explanation enabled Julia and Kevin to take a step back and look at their fights in a totally different way. They immediately identified their anxious and avoidant tendencies, and they could see how these attachment styles influenced the ways they reacted to conflicts with other people and backfired when used with each other. They had been locked in a no-win communication struggle that needed to change. And it did: Kevin now feels more sympathetic to Julia, and she in turn feels more loving toward Kevin after realizing he is as devoted and committed to the marriage as she is.

With this newfound awareness of the toxic effects of the stepcouple shuffle, you may also see both your and your partner's insecurities more clearly. What you used to experience as an attack or a rejection, you will now understand is a way for you and your partner to express an underlying fear of abandonment stemming from childhood scars. Knowing this may change your perception of your partner's personality, as it did for Kevin and Julia.

Feeling more compassion for partners is one healthy outcome of recognizing the negative effects of the stepcouple shuffle, but by itself, it's insufficient to change the way you and your partner fight or how it feels when you fight. Even though Kevin now understood that Julia expressed her anxiety by getting pushy and angry, he thought it would be difficult to keep this in mind when they were fighting. Julia agreed that it would be hard to override her feelings of rejection when he withdrew in the heat of the moment.

The good news is that you and your partner can learn to communicate in a way that does not drive the other away. You can also learn ways to help your partner tune in and respond to you meaningfully. Let's begin to examine how to break free from the stepcouple shuffle and develop kinder, more compassionate communication with your partner. Chapters 9 and 10 will address the first step of the stepcouple shuffle, the anxious partner's approach, and chapter 11 will focus on the second step of the stepcouple shuffle, the avoidant partner's response. The remaining chapters in this section will cover strategies for both types of partners to improve communication. So are you ready to dance to a different beat? Let's go!

9

BOLSTER YOUR
SECURITY LEVEL

Once you recognize and understand the harmful nature of the step-couple shuffle, your perception of several things will change. Most important, you will understand that you and your partner are not incompatible—your *emotional attachment styles* are incompatible. This distinction frees you from blaming each other for your relationship problems. You and your partner aren't intentionally trying to hurt each other when withdrawing or getting angry during conflicts. Rather, your clashing anxious and avoidant reactions end up hurting both of you. This insight enables you to begin the process of forgiving each other for unintentional past injuries and provides a clear path to improve your relationship.

For those of you with anxious attachment styles, there are two primary ways to improve your communication during conflicts: (1) bolstering your security level and (2) modifying your reactions during fights to ensure you aren't affecting your partner's security level. This chapter will look at strategies to help you become more secure.

SLOW DOWN, YOU'RE MOVING TOO FAST

As partners get more and more habituated to the stepcouple shuffle, conflicts escalate and heat up more quickly. For some stepcouples, the pace quickens to the point that one word can trigger an avoidant or anxious reaction, and they are off and "dancing." When this happens, partners miss opportunities to truly understand what each is communicating. To fully express yourself during conflicts, acknowledge each other with compassion, and resolve issues as teammates, you need to better express the feelings that underpin the anger instead of the anger itself.

Even though anxious and avoidant partners express anger differently, the emotion serves the same purpose. Anger protects us after we have been hurt, frightened, or threatened. Our bodies respond physiologically to both perceived and real threats in several ways: our heartbeats race, our breathing rates increase, and our cortisol levels become elevated, priming us for a fight-or-flight response. These were very effective survival responses for our ancestors hundreds of years ago, but they are not useful when fighting with partners today.

One way to avoid the stepcouple shuffle is to dial down angry reactions during conflict. Partners must become more adept at listening to each other's point of view without immediately defending their positions. When I explained to Julia and Kevin that they had to be more patient with each other, Julia said that during a conflict she would bite her tongue as long as she could until finally she would explode in anger, frustrated by Kevin's refusal to participate in the conversation. She didn't think she was capable of fully controlling her anger and wondered why Kevin couldn't just shake off her mean comments when the fight was over. After all, didn't he know how much she loved him and that she was just trying to get a response from him? I explained that for many people, being yelled at or criticized is more painful than being physically assaulted. Not only were her angry outbursts damaging Kevin's self-esteem, they were hurting her as well. He was holding a grudge against her for treating him cruelly and was having trouble forgiving her. Her angry behavior was going to jeopardize their marriage if it did not change.

Julia voiced another concern about curbing her angry outbursts. She saw herself as a passionate and intense person and was afraid that if she controlled her anger, she would lose part of her identity. I explained that I wasn't suggesting she change her personality, but rather encouraging her to express the feelings underlying her angry outbursts, which is actually a more authentic way to express who she is. Next time she was angry with Kevin, I encouraged her to pause and think about what was hurting her and express this, instead of anger.

She admitted that after a fight, Kevin felt more emotionally bruised than motivated to make the changes she wanted. I explained that expressing anger with contempt, by belittling a partner, name-calling, or bullying a partner to change, rarely accomplishes anything positive. In fact, contempt is the most destructive element in communication between couples.[1] It damages both a partner's self-esteem and a couple's emotional connection.

To help reduce your anger and develop more patience, it's important to reduce the amount of overall stress in your life. The more you've got on your mind, the easier it is to lose patience and give in to temptation, whether that be overeating, drinking too much, or lashing out in anger. When your brain is overtaxed, it reacts to events by habit. An effective way to become more patient is for you and your partner to practice mindful meditation on a regular basis.

PRACTICE MINDFUL MEDITATION

Meditation can help you pause before responding to your partner angrily, help you recognize the underlying emotions, and express them productively. Inspired by Buddhist traditions, mindful meditation has many benefits. When practiced regularly, it trains your mind to experience the present moment rather than focus your attention on the past or anxiously anticipate future events that may or may not happen. It helps to regulate your emotions as well as increase body awareness and self-awareness. Studies suggest that those who meditate regularly are happier and more content than those who don't.[2]

Recent evidence suggests that mindfulness actually changes the structure of our brains.[3] When we experience stress, the right prefrontal cortex of our brain, the part that is associated with negative emotions, becomes much more active than the left side. Activity in the amygdala, the region of the brain that responds to fear, also increases during stress. When we meditate, the left prefrontal cortex, the side connected with pleasant emotions and positivity, is activated, and activity in the amygdala decreases. These changes suggest that mindfulness can modulate the way we respond to threats and help us manage stress more effectively.

Meditation is particularly useful if you have anxious or avoidant tendencies because it helps you recognize recurring negative thought patterns. And refocusing your attention on your breath can then prevent you from spiraling into depression or anxiety. Meditation also helps you accept and deal with feelings rather than run away from them or seek to get rid of them by demanding help from partners.

Meditation is very simple. All you do is sit in a quiet place and focus your attention on the physical sensations of your body, such as your breathing, while simultaneously maintaining a sense of relaxation. At first it may be difficult to sit in one spot for 10, 15, or 20 minutes without doing anything else, but over time it becomes much easier—and actually is quite enjoyable.

Try this exercise: find a quiet space to relax. Sit comfortably in a chair with your hands resting in your lap or on your knees. Keep your back straight. Your neck should be relaxed and your chin slightly tucked in. Begin by taking five deep breaths, breathing in through the nose and out through the mouth. On the last exhalation, let your eyes gently close.

Gently observe your posture and notice the sensations of your body. Slowly scan your body from head to toe, observing any tension or discomfort. Now turn your awareness to your thoughts. Notice any thoughts that arise without attempting to alter them. Gently note your underlying mood, just becoming aware of what's there without judgment.

Bring your attention to your breathing. Don't try to change the rhythm, just observe the rising and falling sensation that it creates in the body. Begin silently counting each breath from 1 to 10. When you get to 10, start counting again. While doing this, it's completely normal for thoughts to bubble up. Just guide your attention back to your breath when you realize your mind has wandered.

After counting from 1 to 10 several times, allow your mind to wander. Spend 20 to 30 seconds just sitting. You might find yourself inundated with thoughts or plans, or you might feel calm and focused. Enjoy this opportunity to let your mind simply be. When you're ready, slowly open your eyes.

When you meditate regularly, you may find that you feel slightly detached from your thoughts and feelings. You realize that thoughts are merely thoughts rather than absolute reality. For example, fearing that your relationship will end becomes just a fear rather than a prediction. When perceived in this way, thoughts are no longer as troubling or distressing, and they no longer have the same power to paralyze or frighten you. Thoughts are just thoughts, nothing more. Jon Kabat-Zinn, the psychiatrist credited for bringing mindful meditation to the United States, said, "You can't stop the waves, but you can learn to surf."[4] You may find that after practicing meditation, you are no longer as anxious and fearful as you once were.

Meditation allows you to regulate your emotions and respond less impulsively to triggers. By remaining calm, you can express yourself more clearly and be respectful to your partner. There are a number of other ways to prevent you from losing your temper.

CHOOSE YOUR TIMING CAREFULLY

Sometimes fights are triggered by a comment, memory, or something someone else has done. Many times, though, you can plan when to raise a difficult issue, which will ensure that you and your partner both have time to discuss it. Some couples schedule an agreed-upon time to specifically discuss a contentious topic. Conflicts are more easily resolved when both of you can relax and focus on each other without any interruptions or distraction, so don't initiate a conversation when you are already stressed, rushed, or busy doing something else.

For example, I recommend you don't bring up a sensitive issue before bedtime. There's a strong possibility you may get upset and will be kept awake by discussing the topic late into the night. Consider instituting a rule that my husband and I adopted. We won't bring up a difficult topic after 10 p.m. Before adopting this rule, we fought into the wee hours of the morning and would be exhausted and grumpy the next day—even if we had come to a resolution.

SET THE STAGE

During a serious discussion or disagreement, you and your partner must give each other your undivided attention. Turn off the TV, step away from your computer or phone, and stop folding the laundry, washing the dishes, or doing anything else. You need to look at and pay attention to each other. This may seem obvious, but how often are you pressed for time and trying to finish something while simultaneously fighting with your partner? (And forget about discussing sensitive topics via texts or emails. Messages are too easily misinterpreted.)

RECOGNIZE WHEN YOU'RE
ABOUT TO "DANCE"

When you start to get irritated with your partner, that's the cue to pause and realize that you're moving into the stepcouple shuffle. Rather than jump to, and act on, assumptions that may be wrong, take some deep breaths before responding, which will make you less likely to get angry or run away. Breathing helps keep us calm. We've known this for centuries, but up until recently we didn't know how it worked. New research on mice suggests that the same neurons that control breathing also control the part of the brain that regulates attention, arousal, and panic.[5] This would explain why we hyperventilate when we are anxious and why deep, controlled breathing helps us calm down.

Try this exercise: here is a simple breathing exercise to do when you begin to get upset:

- Breathe through your nose rather than your mouth.
- Slow your breathing down by inhaling to a count of four. Pause for a moment, then continue to exhale by counting to four.
- Keep your breaths as smooth, steady, and continuous as possible. Pay particular attention to exhaling smoothly and steadily.

COUNT TO 10

This old-fashioned technique really works. Delaying your impulse to lash out in anger by just a few seconds can help prevent an angry outburst. To really slow down your desire to express anger, count to 10 in another language. (And if the impulse to explode in anger is really strong, count to 100.)

LISTEN WITHOUT INTERRUPTION

To stop yourself from engaging in the stepcouple shuffle, listen carefully to what your partner is saying and take your time before responding. Don't say the first thing that comes into your head, but think about what you want to communicate. Remember, you don't have to solve the problem immediately. These steps will help you listen without interrupting your partner:

1. Take deep breaths to keep from jumping in before your partner is finished speaking.
2. Allow your partner to finish each point before sharing your opinion or asking any questions.
3. Remain open-minded. When you feel you are becoming defensive, continue to take deep breaths.
4. Don't offer counter explanations.
5. Occasionally nod your head to show you are still listening.

When your partner is finished speaking and it is your turn to talk, make sure you fully understand his point of view by reflecting on what he said. If you're not sure, ask questions to clarify certain points.

FOCUS ON YOUR GOAL

If you find yourself getting upset, remember that your feelings are valid and you should not dismiss or disregard them. However, you don't always have to share them with partners, especially if they will only cause harm. Instead focus on your goal. Julia would have had a better result if she had spoken directly to Kevin about the outcome she sought (getting his son to say hello to her) instead of expressing her anger about his ineffective parenting. She might have said, "Next time I come home, please remind your son to greet me." And he'd be more willing to help than he was when he felt attacked.

TAKE A TIME-OUT

Time-outs aren't just for small children. Taking a short break, 10 to 15 minutes, during a conflict allows you to cool down, lower your heart rate, figure out what is bothering you, and resume the conversation calmly.

These basic, proven techniques help you remain calm during conflicts so you don't participate in the stepcouple shuffle. In the next couple of chapters, we will examine and modify any thoughts that spark insecure reactions.

10

MODIFY YOUR REACTIONS

For those with anxious attachment styles, becoming more secure is an important aspect of improving communication with one's partner. In the last chapter, we covered ways to control anger during conflicts. Changing your thought patterns is another way to help prevent you from getting embroiled in the stepcouple shuffle. In this chapter we are going to learn how to let go of any outdated thoughts, old emotional injuries, and resentments that may negatively color your perceptions of yourself and your partner.

Some of the passing thoughts and beliefs that flow through your mind accurately reflect your reality, while others may no longer be relevant and can alter your everyday experiences without your even realizing it. For example, you may forgo attending a party because you were shy as a child and still believe you are socially awkward despite the fact that you have outgrown your shyness and matured into a gregarious adult. You just don't realize you've changed. You may hold similar inaccurate or outdated views about yourself or your partner that damage communication with each other. While it isn't possible to change past events, you can change your perception of them so that they don't encumber present moments. Letting go of outdated thoughts and beliefs can increase the amount of intimacy and fun you have with your partner.

EXAMINE AND REVISE YOUR BELIEFS

For those with anxious tendencies, here are a couple of beliefs to consider revising:

Table 10.1.   Old Beliefs and New Beliefs

Old Beliefs	New Beliefs
I suffer from low self-esteem.	I am a worthy person.
I resent my partner for hurting me in the past and believe she will hurt me again.	Even though my partner has hurt me in the past, she loves me very much.
I need my partner's help to survive.	I am independent, resourceful, and resilient.

Let's take a closer look at each of these beliefs and how to revise them.

Belief Revision #1

OLD BELIEF: I SUFFER FROM LOW SELF-ESTEEM.

One of the most common beliefs anxious partners hold on to is that they are not worthy. These feelings of low self-esteem are often triggered by an argument. While conflicts with partners are inevitable, getting a sick feeling in the pit of your stomach, worrying that your relationship will end, feeling bad about yourself, and emotionally beating yourself up shouldn't follow a fight. Equally damaging are terrible feelings you might have about your partner after a fight that help you build a case that she is untrustworthy.

After a fight with Kevin, Julia berated herself by inwardly saying she was stupid for even trying to get him to change his parenting style. He'd never listen to her in the past; why would he now? As she put herself down for trying to change Kevin's behavior, she globalized her negative thoughts and told herself she was incapable of doing anything correctly. And because she felt like a failure, she believed she was one. Julia dwelled on these feelings for days after a fight.

While secure individuals don't like to fight with their partners, they recover fairly quickly after a fight and don't harbor negative feelings about themselves, their partners, or their relationships. Most significantly, conflict does not dent their self-esteem.

With strong self-esteem you are more able to remain calm during difficult discussions and control your impulse to engage in the stepcouple shuffle. You need to learn to replace negative self-perceptions with more positive ones and then take supportive actions to reinforce these new thoughts. (Of course, you don't have to do this alone. You can consider going to a psychotherapist or counselor to help improve your self-esteem.) First, let's focus on reframing your self-beliefs.

NEW BELIEF: I AM A WORTHY PERSON.

Try this exercise: To overcome negative self-perceptions, you need to become aware of how you think about yourself. Think back to a fight you had with your partner. Afterward, what thoughts did you have about yourself? These thoughts really make a difference in determining how you feel about yourself and the actions you take. Write them down in a journal and review them. Do they fit into any of these categories?

- *Negative self-talk:* Do you undervalue yourself, put yourself down, or use self-deprecating humor to describe yourself? Do you call yourself stupid or other derogatory names after minor infractions?
- *Perfectionist thinking:* Do you believe you have to be perfect to be loved, and beat yourself up after making any mistakes?
- *All-or-nothing thinking:* Do you believe that if you don't succeed at a task, you are a total failure?
- *Mental filtering:* Do you focus only on your negative attributes and discount compliments from others or reject positive thoughts about yourself?
- *Mistaking feelings for facts:* Do you believe that if you feel like a failure, you are one?
- *Jumping to negative conclusions:* Do you quickly reach a negative conclusion about yourself even though there is little or no evidence to support it?

As you identify the pattern in which you criticize yourself, it's easier to catch negative thoughts as they move through your mind. Then you can reframe them to more positive ones using the tips below.

- **Use hopeful statements.** After catching yourself saying something negative about yourself, add some kind and encouraging words. Pessimistic beliefs don't have to become self-fulfilling prophecies if you neutralize them with positive statements. Instead of saying, *I can't ever say the right thing to my partner*, say, *I will try to explain how I feel to the best of my ability. I am a work in progress.*

- **Forgive yourself.** If you start to feel bad about yourself after making a mistake, tell yourself that everyone makes mistakes, and mistakes don't reflect who you are as a person. They're just isolated moments in time. Tell yourself, *Making a mistake doesn't make me a bad person.*

- **Avoid making statements with "should" and "must."** If you repeatedly tell yourself you *should* love your stepchildren, or you *must* work harder to be accepted by your regenerated family, please understand that you are placing unreasonable demands on yourself. Replace the word "should" with the word "could." *I could work harder to be accepted by my regenerated family.* Eliminating "should" and "must" from your vocabulary can lead to more realistic expectations and ease any feelings of guilt and shame you may have.

- **Postpone feeling upset.** If you feel rejected and insecure after your partner withdraws from a conversation, consider that your feeling stems from an assumption you are making that she doesn't care enough about you to finish the conversation—which may not be the case. (If your partner is avoidant, remind yourself that she also feels bad about fighting with you and needs space to recover.) Try to hold off having a feeling based on assumption. Wait until you know it is a fact before feeling bad. It is likely you are just catastrophizing and feeling worse than is warranted.

- **Encourage yourself.** Give yourself credit when you make a positive change. You are quick to criticize yourself, so be as quick to provide compliments and praise.

- **Celebrate your successes.** Even small ones. Any progress is worthy of celebration. These small cognitive changes can make a big difference with regard to how you feel about yourself.

Belief Revision #2

OLD BELIEF: I RESENT MY PARTNER FOR HURTING ME
IN THE PAST AND BELIEVE SHE WILL HURT ME AGAIN.

You may be an equal-opportunity critic, as judgmental of your partner as you are of yourself. Anxious individuals tend to form resentments of partners who do not acknowledge their needs or express appreciation for their help. Over time, this can build to form a very negative view of the partner.

When your partner hurts you, do you add this to the list of other grievances that you mentally keep? Are you skilled at doing this? I must admit I am, and have been told I should have been a lawyer because of my ability to build a compelling argument. I used to get annoyed when my husband would leave several pairs of shoes by his desk rather than put them in his closet. When I would notice the shoes, I would immediately recall other times he was messy. Rather than continue down this negative path, I realized I could go down a more realistic one. Instead of listing all his past transgressions, I thought about the chores he does around our apartment. Among others, he vacuums—a chore I hate to do and haven't done once since we got married more than 25 years ago. I am very grateful that he does this, and my appreciation for his doing this task and others reduces my annoyance that he does not put his shoes in the closet.

NEW BELIEF: EVEN THOUGH MY PARTNER HAS HURT
ME IN THE PAST, SHE LOVES ME VERY MUCH.

Try this exercise: Do you tend to build a negative case against your partner? Next time your partner upsets you, sit down immediately afterward and write in a journal what you are thinking and feeling. You might be surprised how quickly you begin to form resentments. Then question whether these feelings are accurate. Could they be exaggerations or distortions of the truth? Is it possible that you are not being fair? Instead of building a case against your partner, think about all the good things she does in service of your relationship. Think about the ways she expresses love for you. Write these down. At first it may be difficult to compile a list because your brain will want to focus only on your partner's negative traits and the times you were hurt. With practice, this exercise gets easier and will offset some of the resentments you carry against your partner.

Belief Revision #3

OLD BELIEF: I NEED MY PARTNER'S HELP TO SURVIVE.

Because of their low self-esteem, those with anxious reactions believe they cannot survive without their partners. They believe they *need* their partners to provide comfort and emotional support when they are upset, since they feel incapable of doing this on their own. Because they lack confidence in themselves, they panic and push their partners to resolve problems, and this sets them off on the stepcouple shuffle.

NEW BELIEF: I AM INDEPENDENT,
RESOURCEFUL, AND RESILIENT.

To avoid the stepcouple shuffle during conflicts, anxious partners will benefit from feeling more self-sufficient and independent. To do this, you must change your belief that you cannot handle life's challenges without your partner's help. Then you can adopt new behaviors that will reinforce this new identity. Here's how I helped Julia accomplish this goal.

Julia could not imagine life without Kevin. This was the main reason she was so scared their marriage would end. She realized, however, that by continuing to place pressure on Kevin to soothe her insecurities, she was creating a self-fulfilling prophecy that would force him to leave her for being too demanding and needy. During therapy, Julia realized she had to change from believing that she could not function as an independent adult to believing she could trust herself to deal with any future problems.

To help her see the possibility that she was capable of soothing her own anxieties and could handle life's challenges by herself, I suggested that Julia examine her feelings of dependency. I explained that they were her feelings, rather than facts. Many people survive divorce, death, and other horrible events and so could she. It wouldn't be easy, and I hoped she was never going to be tested, but I knew she could persevere and get through all challenges. I told her about a conversation that changed my perspective about taking care of myself.

When I was younger, I believed the world was divided into two types of people: those who were strong and those who were weak. Only the strong would survive when struck by tragedy or other challenges. The weak would be unable to handle these challenges. Since I didn't feel strong, I was very scared I would crumble when dealing with life's curveballs. This belief changed when I was in graduate school and talked to a classmate, a Vietnam War veteran who explained how wrong I was about categorizing people into two groups. He explained how he developed strength after, not before, being blinded by shrapnel. Before enlisting in the army, he had been a sculptor who won many awards for his work. After he was blinded, he was very depressed and angry that he could not resume this career, let alone see for the rest of his life. His path to recovery was not linear. He had good days and bad days in rehab. Over time, he developed strength, and he learned to function with the assistance of a guide dog. He explained that no one is prepared ahead of time to deal with life's adversities. All of us develop strength as we go along. His simple explanation gave me confidence that while I might face many challenges, I would learn to handle them, just like others have. As human beings, we are resilient. I passed this piece of wisdom along to Julia and hoped it would give her a new outlook on her ability to handle difficulties. I hope it helps you as well.

DEVELOP YOUR CONFIDENCE

It isn't sufficient just to think more positively about yourself—you need to reinforce this new identity by taking actions that build self-confidence. Self-confidence isn't a characteristic that remains fixed throughout our lives. It varies, and it can grow or diminish depending upon our behaviors. When we do things that we regret and feel ashamed of, our self-esteem, and thus our confidence, diminishes. When we take positive actions, it builds. Life is much more enjoyable and our resilience is reinforced when we choose activities that build pride instead of shame and guilt.

Julia was excited about building her self-confidence and asked me what she could do. I told her about the research of Peterson and Seligman, two founders of the positive psychology movement, who identified six virtues and 24 character strengths that are central to good character.[1] They believe that you are more likely to flourish if you use or "flex" positive characteristics that allow you to perform at your personal best, such as curiosity, valor, or generosity. Their research found that people who used one of their strengths in a new way each day for a week were happier and less depressed six months later than those subjects who didn't do this exercise. (The list of Peterson and Seligman's virtues and character strengths can be found in appendix A.) Other researchers found that people who used their strengths were more positive, showed greater vitality, and had improved self-esteem compared to those who did not.[2]

As a way to build confidence, Julia set out to become better rounded. She thought about what she enjoyed doing and decided to take piano lessons, which she had loved as a child. She also wanted to become a better gardener and found a horticulture class to take at her local community center. These activities served three purposes: they distracted her from worrying, they allowed her to have fun and make new friends who shared her interests, and, most important, they boosted her confidence. As Julia's confidence grew, she no longer felt as powerless in her relationship with Kevin.

Try this exercise: What activities do you enjoy and derive satisfaction from? If you're not sure, ask close family members and friends for their opinions about your positive characteristics and interests. Those who know us well often have excellent insights about who we are. Or you can ask yourself these questions to help guide you:

- What activities do I particularly enjoy?
- What activities come naturally to me?
- When do I feel the most authentic?
- What do I pay most attention to?
- What activities do I do without having to remind myself to do them?

Commit to doing one activity that you love every day. This is one way to gain self-confidence and will counteract the negative effects of worrying.

TIPS TO IMPROVE YOUR SELF-ESTEEM AND SELF-CONFIDENCE

Building your self-esteem and self-confidence takes time and practice. These strategies will help you tremendously:

- Make two lists: one of your strengths and one of your achievements. If you have trouble doing this, get a supportive friend or relative to help you. Read through each list every morning to remember your positive qualities.
- Stop comparing yourself to others. Stop comparing yourself to an idealized version of yourself. You are just fine the way you are.
- Pay attention to your personal hygiene: take a shower, brush your teeth, trim your nails, and so on. Wear clean clothes that make you feel good about yourself. Make your living space clean, comfortable, and attractive. You feel good about yourself when you take care of yourself and your home.
- Do some activities that you have been putting off, such as filing paperwork or decluttering your closet and drawers. Start slowly by devoting 10 minutes to the selected task.
- Be creative. Express yourself through writing, painting, music, poetry, dance, or another creative outlet.

Taking time to focus on your personal growth and development will help you feel more secure, and this will help you communicate more effectively with your partner.

11

DON'T LET A GRUDGE
WEIGH YOU DOWN

Relationships improve when anxious partners let go of negative self-perceptions and take actions to become more secure. As they boost their self-esteem and independence, they feel stronger and more powerful, thus responding to their partner in more positive ways during conflicts. They are better able to maintain their composure, and this helps their avoidant counterparts to also remain calm. There's no need to flee from a conflict when an anxious partner isn't demanding help that reaches beyond an avoidant partner's comfort zone. But while this helps, it's insufficient to fully change the way an avoidant partner reacts to conflicts.

To fully stop participating in the stepcouple shuffle, avoidant partners need to modify two underlying beliefs that drive them to withdraw: (1) that independence is more valuable than being in a relationship and (2) that it is better to squash feelings than to discuss them with partners. These two beliefs limit intimacy. It is preferable to perceive partners as teammates rather than adversaries; this improves communication during conflicts and strengthens emotional bonds.

EXAMINE AND REVISE YOUR BELIEFS

If you are avoidant, consider revising the beliefs shown in table 11.1.

Table 11.1.   Old Beliefs and New Beliefs

Old Beliefs	New Beliefs
I value my independence.	My partner and I are teammates.
It is preferable to squash negative emotions.	I don't have to be burdened by past grudges. I can live in the moment, experience all feelings, and tackle problems with my partner as they occur.

Belief Revision #1

OLD BELIEF: I VALUE MY INDEPENDENCE.

The withdrawal step of the stepcouple shuffle is as harmful to a relationship as the approach step. Avoidant partners close the door to intimacy, forgoing opportunities to experience its benefits, such as care, support, and validation from their partners. Not only do they choose to sacrifice opportunities to receive comfort, they do not like to spend time nurturing partners and prefer instead to focus their energies on personal pursuits. They justify this choice by overinflating the importance of their goals while devaluing those of their partners. This choice leaves their relationship vulnerable to withering and dying from neglect.

Are you too independent? Can you relate to these statements?

- You believe your actions only affect you.
- You are a workaholic, and during leisure time you choose to work instead of spending time with your partner.
- You don't like to share. For instance, you prefer to pay household expenses from separate accounts rather than comingle finances with your partner.
- You feel guilty accepting gifts from your partner because you don't like to be bothered with buying gifts for him.
- At times you find it is easier to lie to your partner than to explain the truth.

Kevin could identify with these statements. While Julia depended on Kevin too much, Kevin didn't depend on her enough. Like many others who have avoidant reactions, he viewed dependency as a weakness. Many times he rejected her offers of support because they contradicted his belief that he should take care of all his needs. He also did not believe Julia was capable of providing him with emotional support when he needed it. While it was true that Julia could be fiery at times, she was also very kind and loving. By keeping her at arm's length, Kevin missed out on these wonderful qualities.

Kevin got annoyed with Julia when she asked him for a favor, since it took him away from his activities. He thought about what the favor would cost him in terms of time and effort rather than considering the benefits he would accrue by helping Julia. He did not realize he was depriving himself of the pleasurable feeling one gets after helping a partner. He also did not consider that Julia's gratitude for his help would lead to more affection between the two of them.

Life is tough enough on one's own, so why go it alone when you have a partner who can help? To receive your partner's love and kindness, you need to change your perception of partners as adversaries and instead view them as allies. You must be willing to depend on your partner, to work as teammates, and to realize that you actually thrive more in a relationship than you do alone.

When you form an interdependent union, you do have to give your partner some power to make you happy—as well as to hurt you at times. Opening yourself to this kind of relationship requires a leap of faith and yet is necessary for the health of your relationship.

NEW BELIEF: MY PARTNER AND I ARE TEAMMATES.

Like any other change, becoming more interdependent will take some time. Here are some suggestions to help facilitate this change.

Make a list of what you do by yourself and what you do with your partner. What can you add to the list of activities you do with your partner? What interests do you both enjoy? Establish a designated time each week to spend quality time together and don't let any other demands take you away from honoring this time with your partner.

Another way to become more interdependent is to ask your partner for help, which initially may rub against your independent mindset.

When your partner helps you, savor the feelings of warmth and appreciation, which ultimately will grow to even more affection and love.

Are you as thoughtful of taking care of your partner's needs as you are of your own? When your partner asks for help, are you willing to comply? Next time your partner asks for help, focus on the benefits you will receive from doing this favor instead of thinking about its cost.

We generally bestow random acts of kindness upon strangers. Make small gestures to your partner by bringing him coffee in bed or filling up the gas tank of his car. Phone, text, or email your partner several times each day to show you are thinking about him. Frequent small, kind acts usually please people more than one grand gesture.

You will know you are more interdependent when

- you enjoy giving to and helping your partner,
- you don't feel guilty or in debt to your partner when you receive gifts and other thoughtful gestures from him,
- you and your partner make decisions together, and
- you and your partner spend quality time together.

Belief Revision #2

Now let's look at another avoidant belief that can benefit from modification.

OLD BELIEF: IT IS PREFERABLE TO SQUASH NEGATIVE EMOTIONS.

It's natural to be hurt during a conflict and then defend yourself by getting angry with your partner. Avoidant partners are uncomfortable directly sharing their feelings and choose to passively express them by withdrawing from conversation and withholding intimacy. Whether conscious or not, this is very hurtful to partners and is an unhealthy way to wield power in a relationship. Both you and your partner suffer from the emotional distance you've created.

Many avoidant partners believe it is better to numb negative feelings than to experience their discomfort. Some actually feel superior to those who can't do this and pity anyone who feels emotions intensely or spends time consciously worrying whether a breakup is imminent. Avoidant partners falsely believe that squashing emotions is a healthier way to handle conflict. This could not be more wrong. By suppressing negative feelings, such as anger, resentment, and bitterness, you place both your personal health and the relationship in jeopardy. It is much better to allow yourself to feel the discomfort of negative emotions and to then share them with partners in a constructive manner. Here's why.

When you suppress negative feelings, you are less likely to experience joyous ones. All emotions, negative and positive, become flattened when you actively try to control them. While those with anxious reactions experience highs and lows that require a lot of energy and can be exhausting, those with avoidant reactions miss the brightness of life and don't have as much fun as they could with their partners.

Unfortunately, detaching your emotions from stressful events does not protect you from their negative psychological and physical effects. To cope with stress, many avoidant partners unconsciously turn to maladaptive behaviors, such as drinking alcohol excessively, using mood-altering drugs, eating too much, or smoking too many cigarettes. Over time, these behaviors can turn into habits that harm your health. Do you spend too much time playing video games? Do you drink or eat too much or engage in other addictive behaviors that comfort you when you're troubled? These impulsive behaviors may stem from suppressing negative emotions. You can begin to overcome bad habits by dealing with the feelings that triggered them in the first place.

One of the most harmful outcomes of numbing your feelings is loneliness. By withdrawing from your partner when you're upset, you end up feeling alone, even if you are lying in bed next to him.

The effects of loneliness have been studied extensively in recent years. Researchers found that loneliness increases the hormonal levels of cortisol in the body and that, over a prolonged period of time, high levels can cause anxiety, depression, digestive problems, heart disease, and weight gain, among other problems.[1] Loneliness also can impair cognitive abilities and disturb sleep patterns. As many of you have probably experienced, when fatigued, you become cranky, impatient, and at greater risk for accidents. You may agree with my favorite expression: "The difference between hope and despair is a good night's sleep."

Not only is loneliness bad for your health, it increases your chances of early death. A recent study concluded that loneliness presents a greater health risk than obesity, smoking 15 cigarettes a day, or alcoholism do.[2] It found that the chance of an early death increases 20 percent from obesity, 30 percent from alcoholism, and 45 percent from loneliness, which also increases the chance of dementia in later life by 64 percent. These are pretty good reasons to stop detaching from your feelings, don't you think?

Here's one more reason: when you don't share anger, resentment, frustration, or bitterness with your partner, these feelings build up inside of you, fester, and form burdensome grudges. Dwelling on the times you were hurt holds you hostage to the past and limits your ability to feel love, happiness, friendship, and all life's other joys.

Holding grudges weighs you down, literally as well as metaphorically. An innovative study examined differences between subjects who were induced to forgive and those who weren't.[3] The grudge holders in the study perceived walking up a hill as more challenging and couldn't jump as high as subjects who were induced to forgive. The subjects in the study who were asked to think about a time they forgave someone jumped the highest—about 30 centimeters. Those who were asked to think of a time they withheld forgiveness jumped about 22 centimeters on average. While these differences may not seem significant in real-life situations, they do demonstrate that our perceptions matter. Our thinking impacts our performance and other behaviors.

NEW BELIEF: I DON'T HAVE TO BE BURDENED
BY PAST GRUDGES. I CAN LIVE IN THE MOMENT,
EXPERIENCE ALL FEELINGS, AND TACKLE
PROBLEMS WITH MY PARTNER AS THEY OCCUR.

Are you holding on to a grudge from times in the past when your partner hurt you? While you may not have received the comfort and compassion you needed at that time, a grudge isn't going to heal that emotional wound. Plus, it locks you into victimhood, which robs you of power. If you want to feel more in control of your life as well as free up space in your brain for peace and contentment, consider letting go of any grudges you are holding.

Before letting go of a grudge, you have to know what caused it. Kevin realized he held a grudge against Julia for the times she criticized his parenting style. Being a good father was an essential part of his identity, and he felt she was criticizing the very core of his being. While he understood he wasn't parenting his son to the best of his abilities, he resented and was angry with Julia for constantly pointing it out. But Julia had no idea Kevin was holding a grudge. After a fight, she would apologize for the mean comments she made about him. Kevin would nod his head, but he never told Julia how much she hurt him and that he was forming a grudge that prevented him from trusting her. After a particularly bad conflict, he finally blurted out that he remembered all the other times she yelled at him and that he would leave her if she didn't stop criticizing him.

This revelation was a major turning point for both Julia and Kevin. She recognized that her criticisms threatened their future together. To remain with Kevin, she had to be more mindful of how she expressed her frustration to him. It wasn't acceptable to lose her temper in the heat of the moment. Kevin also recognized he wasn't a total victim and that he shared some responsibility for Julia's outbursts. The more he withdrew, the angrier she became. If he had been willing to continue these conversations with Julia, she would not have lost her temper. Consequently, he would not have been angry and resentful of her for lashing out. Kevin needed to make changes in the way he communicated during conflicts with Julia. He had to stop using the avoidant step of the stepcouple shuffle.

REFRAME YOUR THOUGHTS

Take a moment and think about the past experiences that contributed to the grudge you hold against your partner. Ask yourself the following questions: what did your partner do? Do you bear any responsibility for what happened? Did your avoidant tendencies prevent you from speaking up to defend your position? Is there anything you could have done differently? If something similar happens in the future, what changes can you make to ensure that your needs get met?

Your answers to these questions may give you a different understanding of the times your partner hurt you. Like Kevin, you may realize that along with your partner, you shared some responsibility for hurting yourself. Now imagine other ways you might have reacted. For instance, how might you have voiced your feelings during the conflict instead of withdrawing from the conversation? Once you identify alternative ways you might have responded, you can choose how to behave in the future. This empowers you. You just turned a regrettable moment into one that helps you avoid getting into in the same position again.

FORGIVE YOUR PARTNER

When you acknowledge some responsibility for hurting yourself, you realize your partner was not entirely to blame. This opens the door to forgiving him. Forgiveness is an important aspect of letting go of a grudge because it repairs your relationship and restores your inner well-being. When you forgive a partner (or anyone else for that matter), you benefit the most. You become unburdened from the emotional weight of the grudge, which can be a tremendous relief.

Forgiveness is not so easy. It takes time and effort, as exemplified by the saying "To err is human, to forgive divine." Even though Julia apologized to Kevin for criticizing him, he still found it difficult to forgive her. He thought it might be easier to forgive her if he better understood why she was so critical of him. He asked her why she lost her temper and made such mean comments. She explained she didn't want to be critical and tried to control her emotions, but over time, she felt so misunderstood by and isolated from Kevin that she became enraged and lost control of what she said. Kevin was able to put himself in her shoes and understood how uncomfortable she had been during those conversations. He felt more compassion toward her and understood her frustration and feelings of powerlessness, but he still could not entirely forgive her for attacking him.

Have you tried to forgive your partner by developing more compassion for him, and found that this wasn't enough? You would not be alone. A recent study found that many of us are "forgiveness averse."[4] We have trouble forgiving partners because our fears and concerns are not addressed by compassion alone. The researchers identified three key stumbling blocks you may be experiencing. First, timing may play a role. You may not be ready to forgive your partner because you still are experiencing too much inner turmoil as a result of being hurt. You may need more time for your emotions to settle down before you are ready to forgive him.

Second, you may resist forgiving your partner because you think it lets him off the hook. You would be excusing, overlooking, forgetting, condoning, or trivializing what your partner did if you forgave him, and this would leave you vulnerable to being hurt again. You can overcome this block by feeling stronger and consequently more powerful in your relationship. Consider doing the esteem-building exercises in the previous chapter. When confident, you can establish and enforce boundaries that will protect you from future harm, making it easier to forgive your partner for past mistakes.

Are you concerned you will "lose face" with family and friends if you forgive your partner? Do you imagine you will see yourself as a doormat or pushover if you forgive him? Concern that others won't respect your decision to forgive a partner is the third barrier to forgiveness. To overcome it, you need to recover your own sense of self-respect and self-worth, which were damaged at the time you were hurt. Make a list of traits that you value about yourself. Think about what you can to feel better about yourself. Good friends, therapists, and clergy may be sources of comfort and may help you restore a better self-image. The exercises in both the previous and next chapters also can help you feel better about yourself.

For most of us, it takes time and effort to forgive our partners, yet it's a worthy endeavor.

SHOW GRATITUDE AND APPRECIATION

Appreciation is the antidote to resentment. Two ways to incorporate gratitude and appreciation into your relationship and your life are to keep a gratitude journal and to say thank you often.

Keep a Gratitude Journal

Researchers found several benefits to keeping a gratitude or appreciation list.[5] In one study, subjects were asked to write down five things they were grateful for each week for 10 weeks, while the control group was not given this task. At the end of the study, those who kept the gratitude list felt more hopeful and healthier as well as less depressed and less anxious than those who didn't keep a gratitude list. Interestingly, the more gratitude subjects expressed, and the longer they kept gratitude lists, the more positive they felt. Another study found that people who kept a gratitude list at the end of each day experienced less stress and a greater sense of calm at night and slept better than those who did not keep a gratitude list.[6]

While beneficial for everyone, keeping a gratitude list is particularly helpful for avoidant partners because it can mitigate their dislike of doing favors for partners. Researchers found that those subjects who expressed more gratitude were more likely to help others, experienced more pleasure by helping others, and experienced greater empathy and lowered feelings of aggression.[7]

I highly recommend you keep a general gratitude list and, for the purpose of improving your relationship, I encourage you to keep a separate gratitude list just for your partner. It will help you see your partner in a better light, which will soften your grudge against him. You will be keeping his good qualities fresh in your mind.

Try this exercise: once or twice a week, write three to five things that you appreciate about your partner. Don't just go through the motions by writing down one or two words to describe what you are grateful for. Elaborate. For example, instead of writing down "vacuumed apartment," I wrote, "My husband vacuumed the apartment before our friends came to dinner. He got rid of the cat and dog hair on the floor and couch so they won't have an allergic reaction. This gave me more time to set the table and make the meal. He cares as much about our household as I do." Going into greater detail provides more context when you reread your journal in the future, and this will trigger even more feelings of gratitude.

In addition to listing your gratitude for activities that your partner has done for you, consider what your life would be like without him. For instance, you might write that if you weren't involved with your partner, you would bear the weight of making household decisions on your own, you would be lonely, and you would not have anyone with whom to share your daily experiences.

Say Thank You to Your Partner as Often as Possible

Keeping a gratitude list will make you more aware of what your partner does for you and for your family. But don't keep your appreciation to yourself; instead, express it to your partner. Your partner will enjoy this, and you will benefit from it as well, because it will actually reduce feelings of resentment for what your partner doesn't do. One study on gratitude found that subjects who said thank you to partners after completing a chore felt less resentment toward them for doing fewer household tasks than the subjects did.[8] These subjects also reported more satisfaction with their relationships than those who did not say thank you to their partners.

You may believe it is unnecessary to thank your partner each time she completes a task. After all, it's a responsibility rather than a favor that must be done to maintain your household. However, "thank you" is a simple way to make your partner feel good. My husband and I can attest to this. We split the evening walk of our dog and thanked the other upon returning home. Even though it's a shared responsibility, we appreciated the nights we didn't have to put on our shoes and go out in the hot, cold, or wet weather, and we acknowledged our gratitude to each other.

Get in the habit of saying thank you to your partner after she does something for you or your household. Your partner will realize how much you appreciate that your life is better because of her. When you focus on the positive rather than the negative attributes of your partner, you will both feel better about each other, and your interactions will improve.

These exercises will help you feel less lonely and more connected with your partner. They will help you accept that your partner is someone to depend upon, a teammate who is by your side through good and bad times.

Let's turn our attention now to developing more courage so that communicating with your partner is not so intimidating.

12

GAIN COURAGE TO EXPRESS FEELINGS WITH CONFIDENCE

Many anxious and avoidant partners get drawn into the approach/avoidance steps of the stepcouple shuffle by the smallest of gestures: a partner's disapproving glance, a sigh, or a critical remark that triggers a fear of rejection. Once this "dance" begins, it is only a matter of time before the insecurities of both partners increase and they grow emotionally distant from each other. In addition to reducing your anger and modifying your limiting beliefs, there's one more change you can make to disentangle yourself from the stepcouple shuffle and begin communicating more effectively with your partner: develop more courage to share your innermost thoughts and beliefs with each other.

Many choose to remain silent during conflicts, afraid that they will cause pain to both themselves and their partners if they speak out. While it isn't constructive to blurt out mean and hurtful comments to one's partner in the heat of a fight, it is important to share feelings in as kind and compassionate a way as possible. Certain issues between partners must be discussed in order to be resolved. Time alone won't make them disappear.

Are you afraid to share your opinions with your partner because you believe these differences will tear your relationship apart? Kevin was afraid to tell Julia that he was scared to become more assertive as a parent and that he believed his son was closed to being taught manners and would resent him for beginning to teach them now. If he admitted this fear to Julia, he believed she would lose respect for him and leave him. In fact, the opposite was true. She considered ending their relationship because he withheld his thoughts and feelings from her. She felt isolated from him, starved for an emotional connection. She would have much preferred that he open up to her even if she did not agree with his point of view. If only he had realized sooner the damage his avoidant tendencies were causing to his relationship, he would have committed to doing exercises to build up his courage.

IDENTIFY YOUR FEELINGS

Once you understand the importance of, and decide to share, your feelings, thoughts, and beliefs with your partner, you may find that they are not so easy to identify. When Kevin realized he needed to share his feelings with Julia, he felt like a deer in the headlights, unable to identify or express what he was feeling. Julia also had trouble voicing her innermost feelings. She was comfortable expressing anger and frustration but couldn't articulate deeper, more vulnerable feelings. From the Center for Nonviolent Communication I gave them a list of feelings people may have when their needs are not satisfied, shown in table 12.1. This list also can help you figure out exactly how you feel.

While all my clients are unique, I have noticed that many partners with avoidant tendencies have certain feelings in common: feeling ashamed that they could never please their partners, feeling helpless and paralyzed to even try, and feeling afraid that their partners will see them as failures. Can you relate to the following statements?

> *I'm better off keeping my opinions to myself because my partner will probably think they're stupid or boring.*
> *If I express my real feelings to my partner, she will reject me.*
> *I need to avoid arguing with my partner because I don't want her to get angry or disapprove of me.*

Many of my clients with anxious tendencies also had certain feelings in common. Like Julia, they were very capable of expressing anger and annoyance when they felt their points of view were dismissed or disregarded by partners; however, they struggled to share their innermost vulnerabilities and fears. They believed they would be judged and ridiculed if they admitted these feelings. Have you ever felt this way?

> *I no longer have control of my life. I have no power in my relationship.*
> *I feel so vulnerable. I am scared my partner doesn't love me as much as I love her and will leave me.*

Table 12.1. Feelings When Your Needs Are Not Satisfied

AFRAID	CONFUSED	EMBARRASSED	TENSE
apprehensive	ambivalent	ashamed	anxious
dread	baffled	chagrin	cranky
foreboding	bewildered	flustered	distressed
frightened	dazed	guilty	distraught
mistrustful	hesitant	mortified	edgy
panicked	lost	self-conscious	fidgety
petrified	mystified	**FATIGUE**	frazzled
scared	perplexed	beat	irritable
suspicious	puzzled	burnt out	jittery
terrified	torn	depleted	nervous
wary	**DISCONNECTED**	exhausted	overwhelmed
worried	alienated	lethargic	restless
ANNOYED	aloof	listless	stressed out
aggravated	apathetic	sleepy	**VULNERABLE**
dismayed	bored	tired	fragile
disgruntled	cold	weary	guarded
displeased	detached	worn out	helpless
exasperated	distant	**PAIN**	insecure
frustrated	distracted	agony	leery
impatient	indifferent	anguished	reserved
irritated	numb	bereaved	sensitive
irked	removed	devastated	shaky
ANGRY	uninterested	grief	**YEARNING**
enraged	withdrawn	heartbroken	envious
furious	**DISQUIET**	hurt	jealous
incensed	agitated	lonely	longing
indignant	alarmed	miserable	nostalgic
irate	discombobulated	regretful	pining
livid	disconcerted	remorseful	wistful
outraged	disturbed	**SAD**	
resentful	perturbed	depressed	
AVERSION	rattled	dejected	
animosity	restless	despair	
appalled	shocked	despondent	
contempt	startled	disappointed	
disgusted	surprised	discouraged	
dislike	troubled	disheartened	
hate	turbulent	forlorn	
horrified	turmoil	gloomy	
hostile	uncomfortable	heavy hearted	
repulsed	uneasy	hopeless	
	unnerved	melancholy	
	unsettled	unhappy	
	upset	wretched	

Source: (c) 2005 by Center for Nonviolent Communication, website: www.cnvc.org; email: cnvc@cnvc.org; phone: +1-505-244-4041.

SHARE YOUR FEELINGS

As painful as your feelings may be to admit to your partner, it is important for you to share them. Just remember, you don't have to express yourself perfectly. If you get flustered during a conversation, or don't know what to say, tell your partner you need some time, say 10 or 20 minutes, to gather your thoughts and figure out a response. You are not under a deadline.

Try these exercises: sharing your feelings requires courage. Here are some exercises you can practice to help you develop more strength.

Exercise 1: Overcome Your Worst Fear

Many people hesitate to share their feelings because they anticipate rejection or ridicule. It helps to know that fears rarely turn into realities. Whatever your worst-case scenario is, remember it is just one of many possible outcomes. It's possible your partner could respond to you with openness and honesty. Allow room in your imagination for your best-case result too!

To help reinforce the difference between a fear and reality, consider a topic that you and your partner struggle with. What is it about this topic that makes you afraid to discuss it with your partner? It would be challenging and unfortunate if your worst-case scenario did occur; however, what resources, skills, or abilities do you have to help you cope with this? You are not as powerless as you imagine, given some of those skills. Really, though, how likely is the worst-case scenario to happen? Is another outcome possible? Imagine the best-case scenario. What is a neutral-case scenario? Coming up with these alternative possibilities puts into perspective that your worst-case scenario probably won't happen, and even if it does, there are many ways to deal with the consequences.

Exercise 2: Strike a Power Pose

To gather courage before raising a difficult conversation with your partner, you can do a physical exercise: stand in a power pose.

In a now controversial study, Carney, Cuddy, and Yap had subjects stand in high- and low-power poses, and they measured their levels of testosterone and cortisol—hormones that affect confidence and calmness—before and after they did so.[1] They found that by adopting body postures that convey competence and power, such as standing up straight or opening our arms, both men and women can boost testosterone and lower cortisol levels to help us feel more confident. Conversely, by scrunching up and wrapping our arms around our bodies, crossing our ankles, and lowering our chins or by hiding our hands in our pockets, we can lower testosterone and raise cortisol levels, so we feel less powerful. The researchers concluded that the hormonal changes achieved by standing in a power pose can make us feel more powerful in a very brief amount of time, and this change could lead to longer-lasting gains of increased tolerance for risk and pain and better ability to think abstractly.

These findings have been disputed by a study that tried to duplicate the results by including more subjects than the original study.[2] These researchers did not find any hormonal or behavioral benefits of standing in power poses. However, similarly to Carney et al., they did find that subjects reported feeling more powerful after standing in a power pose. So standing in a power pose may not physiologically change your hormonal levels or cause long-lasting behavior change, but it can momentarily change how you feel. And this may give you more confidence before a difficult conversation with your partner.

Before raising a sensitive topic with your partner, consider standing in a power pose. For two minutes, stand like Wonder Woman with your hands on your hips, feet apart, and chin tilted upward. Another pose you can do is raising your arms above your head in a victory stance. (Some do this in the privacy of their bathroom so they don't feel self-conscious.)

Exercise 3: The Tree Exercise

Visualization can help you attain a goal or change a behavior. Did you know that instead of practicing on the court, many professional tennis players visualize playing an entire game before an important match to prevent injury? Some people visualize how they will look in a dress to motivate themselves to stick to a diet. The tree exercise uses visualization to give you more courage. Sit in a chair, close your eyes, and imagine you are a strong tree, such as a giant oak, with roots that extend far underground. Take a few minutes and visualize yourself as strong, steady, and resolute. No matter how much the wind may blow or how strongly the rain may fall above ground, your roots will protect you from any negative force. Nothing can topple you. This exercise is designed to help us realize we are stronger than we think we are and can handle difficult circumstances.

Exercise 4: Bubbles

Here's one more exercise to help you gather strength before going into any uncomfortable situation. Take a few moments in private. Close your eyes and focus on your breathing. Imagine that with every breath you inhale, you create a bubble of protective energy around you. In this space, only love and strength can enter. You are safe. All negative energy is deflected, unable to penetrate the impermeable bubble and hurt you. Visualize this positive force surrounding you.

Kevin employed each of these exercises before having a conversation with his son, Matt. When he realized he had avoidant tendencies, Kevin suddenly saw his style of parenting through a different lens. He realized his avoidant emotional style prevented him from being the best parent he could be. He now understood Julia's complaint that he was being too lax in refusing to encourage Matt to say hello to her and others. Not only wasn't it unfair to her, he recognized it wasn't fair to expect his ex-wife to be solely responsible for teaching his son good manners; he also had to step forward and teach Matt social skills. Kevin decided that change was long overdue and the first thing he would do was hold a conversation with his son.

Even though Kevin was motivated to talk to Matt, he was nervous about the outcome. He imagined the worst-case scenario—that his son would no longer want to spend time with him. Thinking it through, though, he realized this was highly unlikely, so he decided to proceed. To gather his courage, Kevin first went to his bedroom and stood in the Wonder Woman pose. Next, to gain even more confidence, he visualized himself as strong, steady, and resolute. Finally, he took some deep breaths and pictured himself in a protective bubble of positive energy. Then he went into Matt's room and asked him how he felt about his marriage to Julia. His son said it was okay, responding to this question with his typical brief, noncommittal response. Kevin said he noticed that Matt didn't talk much when the three of them were together, and he never thanked Julia for the meals she prepared and other things she did for him. He wanted Matt to be more comfortable with her and others. Was there anything Kevin could do to facilitate this? Matt said no. Kevin then apologized to his son for not doing as good a job as a parent as he could. From now on, he was going to help Matt develop better social skills by reminding him to say hello to Julia, to answer questions with a sentence rather than a grunt, and to thank her right after she did something for him. Kevin hoped Matt realized he was going to be doing this out of love. He wanted to help Matt participate more in social interactions.

Julia was so happy when Kevin told her about this conversation. She felt he was finally on her team because he took action that benefited their marriage in addition to helping her stepson improve his interpersonal skills. A little communication went a really long way! Julia also took this opportunity to search her soul and identify her underlying fears to share with Kevin. She realized that Kevin was much more open to hearing about her insecurities than he was to experiencing her wrath.

Developing courage helps you share your deepest feelings with your partner, helps you set clear boundaries for those who violate yours, and allows you to do activities that previously scared you.

13

COMMUNICATE EFFECTIVELY

Good communication is considered the most important element in building a loving, intimate relationship. In one study researchers asked more than 2,000 participants to rank seven relationship skills or competencies that marriage and family therapists consider essential: communication, conflict resolution, knowledge of partner, life skills, self-management, sex and romance, and stress management.[1] They found that participants who reported good communication with partners had the highest level of relationship satisfaction.

Effective communication is a two-way process whereby what is said by one partner is accurately heard by the other. In other words, the communicated message is received as intended. For this to happen, both partners must be fully attentive. Otherwise, too many external obstacles, such as a noisy or distracting environment, or more important, the clash of partners' different emotional styles during conflicts, get in the way.

Good communication is not always easy, particularly during conflicts. As you are well aware by now, the approach/avoidance steps of the stepcouple shuffle—fueled by hurt feelings that turn to anger—along with outdated relationship beliefs prevent partners from communicating effectively during conflicts. Hopefully, the exercises in the last few chapters have helped address those issues. You may now be wondering how to clearly express your thoughts and feelings and listen to your partner in an unbiased way during conflicts. Here are a few pointers that will help you both get your points across.

STICK TO THE POINT

Many times "less is more" when discussing an upsetting topic. While you may be tempted to address everything that is bothering you or make your case by giving every past example you can think of, your partner probably will get bored or defensive by the time you get to your point. When you give too much background information, your main message becomes diluted, and chances are, you won't accomplish your goal. Instead you end up just making your partner feel bad about himself after hearing about all the times he did something wrong.

Julia provided too much detail when talking to Kevin about a problem. She believed she had to present a strong argument to convince him to transform his lax parenting style to a more assertive one. So she described multiple occasions when he did not remind Matt to respond to her questions. Instead of bolstering her cause, she harmed it. The more examples she gave, the more he resented her for criticizing her parenting ability, and he grew more stubborn and less willing to give her what she asked for. If she had kept her requests simple, she stood a much better chance of having Kevin remind Matt to answer her questions at dinner.

Julia had another habit that annoyed Kevin. During a disagreement, she would correct his perception of past events. For instance, if he claimed that he did remind his son to answer her question, she would tell him he was wrong and describe what actually took place at those times. She believed if she provided an accurate portrayal of the past, Kevin would have an aha moment, radically change his point of view, and be more willing to change his parenting style. Unfortunately, this strategy is ineffective. Even if Kevin accepted her version of past events as factual, his feelings about them would not change. Inadvertently, Julia wasted a lot of energy by rehashing the past.

Do you provide too much information to your partner when requesting a change in his behavior? Before bringing up a sensitive topic with him, think about your ultimate goal. To help you stay on track, write it down beforehand.

USE "I" MESSAGES

When Julia was upset, she looked to Kevin to feel better. She believed only he had the power to make her happy. And her words reflected this belief. For example, she would say, "At dinner tonight, you didn't remind Matt to answer my questions." Kevin didn't hear this comment as a plea for help; instead he heard it as another example of how he was a bad parent and a disappointing husband.

Julia's use of pronouns is another example of the importance of carefully choosing your words. To communicate her request more clearly and avoid hurting Kevin, Julia could have changed the pronoun she used from "you" to "I." She could have said, "I feel hurt when your son doesn't answer my questions. I feel like an invisible ghost who doesn't matter." While using the "I" point of view is a subtle distinction in re-phrasing a belief or request, it's less accusatory. It sparks less defensiveness from your partner and helps him be more responsive to your message.

LAYER CONFLICTS WITH KINDNESS

Even if it's not easy, be kind to your partner during conflicts. When hurt and angry, it's often hard to remember that you love your partner and need to treat him with respect. Your first instinct may be to attack him for hurting you. Or, like Julia, you may be itching to point out your partner's mistakes. Try to curb these impulses. You can never justify cruelty to your partner by believing "the truth hurts" or by rationalizing that it's acceptable to give your partner a taste of his own medicine. It may require some thought and mental rehearsal, but you can find a way to be diplomatic and still be honest.

No one likes to be hurt, and it is natural to want to protect our-selves. However, our reactions to partners may be less harsh if we accept that they aren't perfect, and at times they will be insensitive to our feel-ings or make mistakes that hurt us. This concept is particularly difficult to accept for those with perfectionistic tendencies who find it challeng-ing to accept their own flaws, let alone their partners'. But by accepting your limitations, you will have an easier time accepting your partner's. Instead of beating yourself up when you make a mistake, consider treat-ing yourself with more kindness—you will have an easier time being kind to your partner when he hurts you.

When you desire to attack your partner for hurting you, instead of expressing anger, share the feeling you had before it. Remember, anger is a secondary emotional response that follows hurt, fear, or disappointment.

Share one of these feelings. The more vulnerable you are, the more likely your partner will respond to you in an open manner, admit his mistake, and apologize.

TAKE RESPONSIBILITY FOR YOUR MISTAKES

After a fight, how long does tension between you and your partner last? Does it go on for minutes, hours, or days? The sooner you recover from a fight, the better it is for each of you and your relationship. Since it takes two to do the stepcouple shuffle, each of you shares some responsibility for the ongoing conflict and has something to apologize for. Apologizing to your partner is an effective way to defuse tension and restore harmony between you. It demonstrates your maturity and often inspires your partner to apologize to you.

After a fight, Julia would analyze what happened and think about the mistakes she made. She would quickly apologize in a heartfelt way for hurting Kevin and promise to be more considerate of his feelings in the future. Kevin had more trouble apologizing to her. He might say, "I'm sorry you felt that way" or "I'm sorry you were hurt," but he wouldn't take direct responsibility for causing her pain. He resisted saying, "I'm sorry I hurt you by giving you the cold shoulder" because he felt inadequate after making an apology. Like many people, his self-esteem plummeted after he admitted to a mistake.

It's possible to maintain one's self-esteem while apologizing, however. One recent study had 98 adults take a survey ranking their values and personal qualities.[2] Afterward, half of the participants were asked to briefly describe why their highest-ranked values were important to them, while the other half weren't given this task. Then both groups were told to think of a time when they had hurt someone else but had not apologized, and to write down what they would say to that person if they were going to apologize. As you might predict, the group that was asked to think about their values wrote better, less defensive apologies.

Try this exercise: before you apologize to your partner, think about something meaningful in your life, such as your career, a skill, a creative hobby, or your participation in an organization. This will help you realize that your life is multidimensional and your self-worth derives from several sources, extending beyond the one mistake you made. When you see your life in a wider perspective, you will feel less defensive about admitting your mistake and better able to make a direct apology.

According to research a good apology includes[3]

- an admission you made a mistake,
- an expression of remorse by taking responsibility ("I'm sorry I hurt you"),
- an offer to repair the damage you caused, and
- a request for forgiveness.

Consider including a few additional elements in your apology.[4] You may want to explain the underlying reasons for your words or actions, promise to behave better in the future, and acknowledge that you understand how your partner was hurt. However, there are a few points you want to be sure to exclude. Do not

- justify your words or behavior,
- make excuses,
- blame your partner, or
- minimize the consequences of your words or actions ("It was just a joke!").

In a nutshell, partners who communicate effectively

- confidently bring up and discuss sensitive topics,
- are direct, rather than passive-aggressive,
- are respectful of their partners at all times,
- confide in partners more than anyone else,
- treat each other kindly, and
- patiently listen to each other.

These past few chapters contained exercises to help increase your security level. The next couple will identify ways to help you boost your partner's security level.

14

BOOST YOUR PARTNER'S SECURITY

Fortunately, attachment styles established in the first year of life are not permanently fixed. As shown in the last few chapters, partners with anxious and avoidant tendencies can become more secure in their relationships. Even better, you don't have to do all the work on your own—you and your partner can help boost each other's feelings of security. If you understand each other's emotional attachment style, you can adjust or "buffer" your reactions during conflicts.[1]

As you probably can surmise, different buffering techniques are needed to help anxious or avoidant partners become more secure. You can ease an anxious partner's insecurities by reassuring her with clear demonstrations of your love and support during conflicts, while you can reduce an avoidant one's fears by ensuring that her autonomy or independence is not threatened.[2] Not only is it possible to ease a partner's fears at the time of a conflict, your efforts can also increase a partner's overall sense of safety and security in the long term too. First, let's discuss how to do this with anxious partners.

There are three primary ways to ease an anxious partner's insecurities during a conflict:

- Convey your love and respect to your partner through your words and actions.
- Provide your partner with emotional support by attentively listening to and responding to her with compassion.
- Prioritize your partner's requests as important to fulfill as your own needs.

By taking these actions, you will demonstrate your commitment to your relationship, build your partner's trust, and strengthen her feelings of security. Seems pretty simple, yet isn't always so easy to accomplish—particularly when you have avoidant reactions.

USE REASSURING STRATEGIES

Have you tried to reassure your anxious partner? In the past you may have tried to comfort her but grew frustrated and gave up after your efforts didn't seem to work. Perhaps you immediately got annoyed when your partner sought your reassurance because you didn't think it was your responsibility to alleviate her anxiety. Or you refused to tell your partner during a conflict how much you love her, as you believed your love should be obvious. Have you noticed that when you ignore or express annoyance to your partner at the times she asks for help, her insecurities increase? If your reaction can damage your partner's sense of security, consider the fact that it can also repair it. So what are some specific ways to boost your partner's feelings of safety and security?

Choose Your Words Wisely

Most of us don't spend a lot of time thinking before we speak and don't realize the impact our words can have on our partner's security level. Here's an example of this. Remember that Julia was very upset with Kevin when one night at dinner he told his son Matt, "I'm on your team." To Julia, this statement indicated that Kevin was keeping her outside the inner circle he maintained with his son. Just one pronoun, the word "I," hurt Julia. If Kevin had said, "We are on your team," she would not have felt excluded. After this dinner conversation, Julia noticed the pronouns Kevin used in sentences when they were fighting and found he used singular pronouns, such as "my son" and "my home," more frequently than plural ones. This heightened her fears that Kevin was not as invested in their relationship as she was.

Julia's reaction is not unique. Researchers examined couples who spent 15 minutes discussing a topic they'd previously identified as an area of conflict while sensors monitored their skin temperature, pulse, heart rates, and physical movements.[3] Afterward, a computer counted the number of times they used "I" and "we" types of pronouns. Couples who used singular pronouns, such as "I," "you," or "me," reported marital dissatisfaction. By comparison, the ones who used words such as "we," "us," and "our" displayed more affection to each other and experienced less stress during disagreements. Researchers concluded that one partner's use of singular pronouns places the other one in an adversarial position. Partners can more easily cooperate with each other when using "we" pronouns in sentences.

This is one more example of the importance of pronoun usage. In the last chapter, I suggested you use the "I" point of view to take responsibility for your feelings or desire to change a behavior rather than blame or criticize your partner by using the pronoun "you." When discussing anything mutual, use "we" instead of "I."

Try this exercise: For the next few days, monitor the pronouns you use when talking to your partner. Do you tend to use singular or plural pronouns when describing possessions? Do you say "my home" or "our home"? Next time you have a conflict, observe which pronouns you use. If you find you use singular ones, you may be experiencing negative feelings toward your partner. Take a time-out to get calm before resuming the conversation. Then switch to using "we" pronouns. This can put you and your partner back on the same team.

Show Physical Affection

When reassuring an anxious partner with words of love and support, you can strengthen your message by lightly touching your partner on the shoulder or arm. Believe it or not, a small gesture, such as a tap on the shoulder, can reinforce your message and make it more difficult for your partner to dismiss your words as insincere or false. Other forms of physical affection, such as holding hands or putting your arm around your partner, can also ease your partner's insecurities. Besides providing mutual physical pleasure, sex is another way to demonstrate your emotional availability as well as strengthen your partner's trust that you love and care about him or her.

Follow Through on Your Words with Actions

The words you use during a conflict aren't the only factors that raise or lower your partner's level of security. Your behavior afterward also counts. Do you consistently follow through with what you promised your partner you would do? Not only is following through on your promises an important way to maintain good self-esteem, it also shows your partner that you are reliable and trustworthy.

To placate an upset partner and end a fight, avoidant partners will often agree to change a behavior or do a task that they have little intention of doing. For example, Kevin would reluctantly agree to have a conversation with Matt about being more mindful of saying hello and goodbye to Julia. However, he never did. After asking for it numerous times, Julia didn't trust that Kevin would fulfill his promise. She concluded he didn't care about her; otherwise, he would have talked to his son. Kevin's lack of follow-through heightened her insecurities. To prevent this, he had some choices: he did not have to agree to talk to Matt, an activity he dreaded. He could have admitted to Julia he was too uncomfortable and scared to have this kind of conversation. Or he could have agreed to have the conversation and then done it. By choosing not to follow through, he undermined Julia's security.

To protect your partner's security during fights, use your words thoughtfully and precisely. Make sure they indicate what you actually intend to do, and then follow through. Don't make promises you can't keep. By consistently demonstrating to your partner that you can be counted on, over time, she will become more trusting and will feel more secure with you.

REMEMBER: SILENCE IS NOT ALWAYS GOLDEN

While words can either boost or decrease a partner's level of security, silence can also have a big impact on it. Inadvertently, Kevin increased Julia's insecurities by withdrawing into his shell every time she made another request. For example, she wanted Kevin to ask Matt to sit in the back seat when they went on car trips. Her stepson would run to the car and scramble into the passenger seat. He seemed to believe the first one who got to the front seat could sit in it. She felt it was a sign of respect to let adults sit in the passenger seat. Plus, she wanted to be able to talk to Kevin during car rides, which was hard to do from the back seat because Kevin and Matt liked to listen to loud music while driving.

At first Julia passively sat in the back seat, too uncomfortable to mention to Kevin that she wanted to change places with Matt, but she eventually asked him to tell his son to sit in the back. Kevin balked at her suggestion and said nothing. Eventually he suggested that he trade places with Julia. He would sit in the back seat while she drove the car. Julia was dissatisfied with this solution, because it wouldn't teach her stepson to respect her as an adult and she still wouldn't be able to talk to Kevin. Julia repeatedly explained her reasoning, hoping that Kevin eventually would understand it and agree to talk to Matt. But the more she appealed to him, the more he stonewalled or gave her the silent treatment, which Julia assumed meant he thought she was being silly and unreasonable. Julia would end up feeling more insecure than before she brought up this topic.

Why was Kevin silent? He interpreted the request as a criticism of him as a parent and husband and unconsciously got back at Julia by punishing her with silence. On a scale of 1 to 10 (with 10 as the most critical), he believed Julia was criticizing him at a level of 9 or 10. While it is true Julia was criticizing his style of parenting and was upset that he wasn't supporting her in the way she wanted him to, she wasn't suggesting he was a bad parent or husband. If she had to rank her level of criticism toward him, it would have been a 1 or 2, so she was surprised by his sharp reaction. In her mind her request didn't warrant such a strong defense, so she grew even more convinced he no longer loved her.

Kevin assumed his interpretation of Julia's remarks was accurate. Many of us also assume that what we infer from our partners' remarks is what they intended to communicate, and then treat our assumption as though it is a fact. Before reacting defensively to what you think your partner is saying, ask if this is what she meant to communicate. I suggested that Kevin say something like "I'm upset because I believe you are suggesting I'm a bad parent. Is this true?"

Kevin was well aware of the protocol that adults sit in the passenger seat and children in the back. Yet he had another reason for withholding this information from Julia. He believed if he agreed with her, he would be renouncing Matt in her favor. He didn't want to be disloyal to his son. But Julia did not want him to choose her over Matt. She just wanted Kevin to understand her viewpoint and then to act accordingly. When he didn't agree with her reasoning, he conveyed the impression that her request was crazy and ridiculous, which made Julia wonder if he was going to leave her because he no longer cared about her.

After I pointed out to Kevin that he heightened Julia's insecurity by keeping silent when she asked to sit in the passenger seat, he felt bad. He told her he knew it was appropriate for adults to sit in the passenger seat, and her request was reasonable. He added that he was scared Matt would feel rejected if he told him to sit in the back seat. He didn't want to hurt him. Kevin asked her to be patient a bit longer. He was waiting for an opportune moment. This satisfied Julia. She felt relief when Kevin validated her feelings.

As Julia grew more secure from doing self-esteem-building exercises, she realized she didn't have to rely on Kevin to tell Matt to sit in the back, and that she could just as easily do it herself. She had hesitated to have this conversation with Matt because she worried that he would resent her, but she realized she couldn't control what he thought of her. As long as she made her request politely and clearly, she could share her thoughts and feelings with him.

ACKNOWLEDGE YOUR PARTNER'S FEELINGS

Inadvertently, Kevin hurt Julia's feelings by ignoring an important step in their conversation: communicating that he understood how and what she was feeling. While you may have the urge to withdraw from a conversation with your partner or dismiss her feelings as inconsequential, remind yourself that you can boost your partner's security if you listen to what she is saying and respond in a way that demonstrates understanding. The power of feeling understood cannot be underestimated. It eases emotional pain and can make the most unbearable situations manageable when you know someone truly gets what you are going through.

Remember, by expressing your understanding, you are not agreeing with your partner's thoughts and beliefs. You are merely conveying that you understand her point of view. Here are some simple steps to follow:

1. When your partner brings up a sensitive topic, first take some deep breaths to help you remain calm. Be patient and don't interrupt. Your partner has a valid perspective that deserves to be listened to. You'll get an opportunity to express your view in a little while.

2. As your partner speaks, try to put yourself in her shoes and then share what you imagine she is thinking or feeling. Kevin might have said to Julia, "I hear you feel left out of our conversation when you're in the back seat. You also feel ashamed to be in the back; your rightful place as an adult is in the passenger seat. Is this correct?" Be sure to ask your partner if your interpretation is accurate and if she feels understood. When you express understanding with empathy, your partner will be reassured of your love.

3. Try not to get defensive. Remember that your partner is not attacking you when making a request or discussing a problem with you. She is just seeking your help, so there's no need to retaliate.

4. After listening to your partner, think about and take responsibility for your contribution to the problem. When Kevin stopped defending himself against the criticism of being a bad parent, a charge Julia wasn't accusing him of, he was able to listen to her appeal and admit why he was preventing Julia from trading places with his son. He told her, "I have been scared to tell my son to move to the back seat. I'm afraid he will feel rejected. Even though I know it's the right thing to do, I'm not comfortable asking him to move just yet."

5. End the conversation with a comment about how much you love your partner. Kevin said, "I love you very much, Julia. I hope you know my reservations about asking my son to move to the back seat have nothing to do with how much I love you." A little reassurance goes a long way to ease a partner's fears of abandonment and rejection during sensitive discussions.

When you acknowledge what your partner is saying, remember that all you have to do is listen. Oftentimes your partner just wants to share her feelings and feel understood. She doesn't necessarily want your help with solving a problem. If you're unsure what your partner actually wants, ask whether she is looking to vent or would appreciate your help in brainstorming ideas to solve an existing problem.

RESPOND TO YOUR PARTNER'S BIDS FOR CONNECTION

Conflicts aren't the only situations where you can ease a partner's fear. Responding to your partner each time she tries to connect with you can also bolster her sense of security. This may not be as easy as it appears, since there are so many ways your partner may try to get your attention during any given day. Your partner may ask you a question, make a comment or joke, smile, wink, give you a knowing look, touch your arm, or text or call you, among many other ways. It can be difficult to respond to each one—especially when you have avoidant tendencies.

If you are avoidant, you probably cherish your privacy and do not like to be disturbed when you are working, reading, watching TV, or doing other activities. Have you ever ignored your partner because you were so engrossed in what you were doing you blocked out what she was saying? Or have there been times when you heard your partner ask you a question or make a comment but deliberately chose to ignore her, hoping this would give your partner the message you don't want to be disturbed? Have you ever told your partner to leave you alone because you're too busy focusing on something else?

When a partner attempts to connect with you and you don't respond, whether you intend to or not, you are rejecting her. The more you do this, the more insecure your partner will feel. These brief moments, or "bids for attention," may seem insignificant, but they have a big influence on relationship satisfaction.[4]

Dr. John Gottman has conducted extensive research on the quality of marital relationships and distinguishes between two types of couples, "the masters" and the "disasters."[5] The masters respond to each other's bids for attention more than 85 percent of the time, while the disasters only respond a third of the time. Gottman found that couples who turn *against* each other's bids for connection by arguing, criticizing, or being sarcastic with each other often get divorced. They don't get divorced as quickly, however, as those couples who turn *away* from or ignore their partner's attempts to get their attention. While it's not ideal for partners to respond negatively to each other, any connection can make a difference, and not responding at all to a partner's bid for attention is more harmful to a relationship than a critical response. When a partner tries to make a connection and gets rejected, over time she accepts a partner's indifference or rejection and gives up on trying to rebid, leading to greater emotional disconnection, and often eventually divorce.

Turning toward your partner leads to a strong emotional connection and is a powerful way to boost an anxious partner's feelings of safety and security. Here are a few suggestions for how to positively respond to your partner:

- Stop what you are doing and, if possible, look your partner in the eye. Maintaining eye contact lets your partner know you are paying attention.
- Respond to your partner as quickly as possible. If you can't respond immediately, tell your partner when you will be able to, and stick to your time frame.
- Don't multitask while responding to your partner. As mentioned previously, it's not possible to listen to and respond to your partner while you continue to read, watch TV, or type a text or email. Your partner will feel unimportant if you are not giving her your full attention.
- Although sometimes a response can be lengthy, most often it can take just a few seconds, and then you can return to what you were doing. You can just shake your head in acknowledgment, make a sound like "uh-huh," or even raise your hand to positively acknowledge what your partner has said.

If you demonstrate to your partner that her needs are as important to you as your own, her security will grow.

15

GO GENTLY INTO CONFLICT

Generally, the Golden Rule, "Do unto others as you would have them do unto you," is a good principle for stepcouples to follow. During conflicts, though, this rule doesn't apply to partners with different attachment styles. Each one needs something different to alleviate distress and feel safe and secure. Partners with anxious tendencies are comforted when they are reassured that they are loved, as we discussed in chapter 14, but partners with avoidant tendencies need something else: reassurance that their independence and autonomy won't be threatened. By "buffering" or adjusting your reactions in a few ways, you can keep your avoidant partner's anxiety level within a manageable range and thereby eliminate the need for him to take the avoidant steps of the stepcouple shuffle.

In a series of experiments, researchers videotaped and then analyzed the interactions of married couples who took turns discussing a trait or behavior they wanted the other one to change.[1] They theorized that this kind of conversation triggers an avoidant partner's fear of losing his or her independence. As predicted, they found that avoidant individuals responded with greater anger and unwillingness to change their behaviors than secure or anxious participants. However, they reacted with less anger when their partners used a gentle approach, conveyed appreciation for the efforts undertaken on their behalf, gave practical support, and reassured their partners that they were capable of handling a given situation. In short, the research underscored that to feel safe and secure during a conflict, avoidant partners

- respond to a gentle approach,
- appreciate practical rather than emotional support,

- need to be told that their efforts are appreciated, and
- want reassurance that they are capable of handling the situation.

HOW TO HAVE A GENTLE CONFLICT

In line with the above-mentioned research, the following strategies will help you to engage in gentle conflict with your partner.

Use the Carrot Not the Stick

One study found that discussions between couples went a lot more smoothly if partners responded to avoidant partners by softening their communication.[2] Unfortunately, this is not so easy for anxious partners to do; they tend to do the opposite by digging in and making demands. Hoping to avoid conflict, they hold their tongues about a problem until they finally explode in frustration; then they often have an outburst, which begins with a demand that their partners change an attitude or behavior. If partners don't immediately agree to their request, they tend to become more insistent.

This certainly applied to Julia. The more she appealed to Kevin to change his parenting style, the louder and shriller her voice became. Kevin experienced this as a form of aggression and feared Julia wanted to control his actions.

Kevin, like other avoidant partners, is hypersensitive to others' negative emotions, including angry tones, sarcasm, and tears. While you might think a partner's tears would arouse empathy, they can trigger a fear of being manipulated, which prevents an avoidant partner from comforting a crying one. Avoidant partners aren't being insensitive to a partner's pain but instead are trapped between compassion and this fear; they can't soothe their partners when experiencing both feelings simultaneously. Consequently, they don't do anything.

Once threatened, it's hard for avoidant partners to think straight. The minute Kevin felt threatened by Julia's anger, his brain froze and he was unable to consider why she wanted him to be more hands-on as a parent. His response is universal: parts of our brains shut down when we feel threatened, and we can no longer process what others are telling us. A recent study examined what happens to people when they are confronted with opinions that contradict their own.[3] The researchers recorded the brain activity of pairs of subjects who were asked to make financial decisions together. They found that when couples disagreed, their brains were less able to process information presented by the other. However, when pairs of subjects agreed with each other, their brain activity indicated that they were able to encode the information provided by the other.

What does this study suggest for stepcouples? In a nutshell, you can't change your partner's mind by making demands or arguing with him. First you have to find common ground. Unfortunately, Julia had no idea her tone of voice scared Kevin because he didn't say anything or indicate with his facial expression that he was fearful of losing his independence. If she had known, she could have tried to modulate her tone to protect his sense of security.

What happens to your voice during a conflict with your partner? Next time you bring up a sensitive topic with your partner or have a disagreement, check your tone. Is there an edge to it? If so, take some deep breaths to relax your throat and vocal cords to soften your tone.

You may think it's disingenuous to mask your feelings by keeping your voice neutral during a conflict. After all, it's important to communicate with your partner as honestly as possible. Like you, I used to believe that my tone should match my feelings to provide others with a clear message. What I found, however, was that my message was lost when my tone of voice was angry or edgy. Instead of reinforcing my message, my tone overrode it. Others responded solely to my tone and became defensive. This sidetracked the conversation, which left me more frustrated than ever.

Avoidant partners tend to feel more secure when discussing problems in an intellectual or rational manner. In a study with married couples, researchers found that avoidant individuals responded with less anger to a discussion of a personal problem when their partners spoke in a direct, matter-of-fact, rational manner rather than getting emotional.[4]

You may find that maintaining your composure during a fight is easier said than done. Most anxious partners want to express negative feelings to partners for two reasons: they want to release their unpleasant feelings, and they hope partners will help them feel better. It takes a lot of self-restraint to control this desire and find other ways to self-soothe during a conflict.

However, doing so can make a big difference in making your partner more at ease with you. And you may derive an additional benefit of becoming more secure by acting in a more secure manner.

Don't Nag

Besides getting louder during a fight, Julia kept repeating her request, hoping further explanation would convince Kevin to change his behavior. Kevin understood her request the first time. The more she nagged, the more he refused to budge. Julia did not intend to nag Kevin but wanted him to simply acknowledge he understood what she was saying. While she preferred he agree to her request, she could handle a refusal. What she couldn't accept was his lack of response, and this drove her to repeat herself until Kevin responded.

As was the case for Julia, nagging can have an effect opposite of the goal you want to achieve. A little nagging is unavoidable in any relationship, but too much annoys avoidant partners. (And those with other styles too. Let's face it—nobody likes to be nagged.) They become more resistant to changing their minds or behaviors.

Next time you ask your partner to change a behavior, make your request just once. Remember that your partner probably understands what you want, so you don't need to provide a lengthy explanation. Ask your partner how he feels about your request and ask for an idea of what you can reasonably expect to happen. Encourage a back-and-forth of ideas. Avoidant partners are less likely to become fearful of losing their independence when there is a normal flow of give-and-take in the conversation.

Start with a Statement of Love

Another way to soften communication with partners is by beginning sensitive conversations with a gentle introduction. A positive statement, or "softened startup," sets the scene and increases the likelihood of a better resolution for a contentious topic.[5]

For example, Julia might have prevented Kevin from feeling threatened had she begun the conversation by saying, "I love you, Kevin, and don't want to upset you. I know how much you love Matt, and I don't want to harm your relationship with him. I know you're scared this will happen if you suddenly become more assertive. I don't want you to do anything drastic. But I feel so bad when he doesn't acknowledge my presence. Next time this happens, could you please say, 'Say hi to Julia'? I don't think this will change his feelings for you, and I would appreciate it so much. Thank you."

Be Polite and Appreciative

If you noticed, Julia's request included phrases such as "please" and "thank you." Just because you are upset with your partner during a conflict doesn't mean you should abandon good manners. This is a time when respect and politeness are especially helpful in maintaining a warm feeling between you. However, in the heat of the moment, many of us lose control of our emotions and say mean things to partners that we would never utter to anyone else. As stated previously, partners can be hurt by these comments, remember them, and have trouble forgiving us even if we didn't really mean what we said. Take deep breaths to control your emotional reaction to partners during conflicts.

Acknowledge Your Partner's Sacrifice

Julia's request also showed an awareness of the effort it would take for Kevin to change his behavior. One research study hypothesized that avoidant partners feel their independence may be jeopardized when they're asked to make a major sacrifice.[6] They assume that if they give an inch, their partners will end up taking a mile. To prevent your partner from fearing you will take advantage of his good nature, express that you understand and appreciate the effort he is making on your behalf. This statement will help your partner understand that you respect his independence.

Express Confidence in Your Partner

Most avoidant individuals exude a quiet calmness, which partners mistake for a sign of confidence. In some situations they are confident, but there are other instances—especially when avoidant individuals are asked to help their partners (or others) with a problem—that they are uncertain if they are up to the task. You partner will feel better if you express confidence in his ability to do the chore. Julia might have bolstered Kevin's confidence by saying, "I know you can teach Matt to be more social. You are already such a good parent."

Provide Practical Assistance

Conflicts are not the only situations in which you can help your partner feel safe and secure. At times, avoidant partners need advice and support. While anxious ones are comforted by kind words, hugs, and other reassuring gestures, avoidant partners prefer practical assistance or suggestions for solving a problem.

When Kevin had a problem at work, he liked to talk about it with Julia. At first, she would tell him everything was going to be okay, words of reassurance that soothed *her* anxiety. Kevin felt these words were platitudes that did not reduce his distress. When Julia realized he preferred to discuss different options for handling the situation, she was happy to comply. She had a lot of experience dealing with difficult, uncooperative coworkers. Julia shared what worked for her but did not tell Kevin what to do. When allowed to make his own decision, Kevin felt self-reliant and retained personal control.

In summary, use the following suggestions to help manage an avoidant partner's anxiety during conflicts:

- Take a gentle approach when asking a partner to change a behavior or opinion.
- Keep your voice neutral and maintain an optimistic tone.
- Encourage conversations with back-and-forth communication.
- React in a calm, forgiving, and supportive manner during a conflict.
- Give practical rather than emotional support.
- Respond with comments that are sensitive to a partner's autonomy needs.
- Acknowledge and appreciate a partner's efforts and convey that you value your partner.

HOW TO GENTLY HANDLE AVOIDANCE

What do you do if these approaches don't work and your partner gets upset and withdraws from you during a conflict? First, remind yourself that withdrawing may be the only way your partner knows how to let go of negative feelings. He isn't withdrawing to reject you or place your relationship in jeopardy but instead is trying to regain his equilibrium.

Give Your Partner Space

If your partner withdraws from you, don't run after him and insist that you finish the fight. Give him space to calm down. This may be difficult for you if you are anxious, but your partner will be grateful for space to calm down. It will demonstrate your respect for his need for independence and prove you have no intention of taking it away from him. Slowly your partner will begin to trust you more.

While giving your partner space, take some time to calm yourself down if you are upset. Take some deep breaths, meditate, or soothe yourself with positive self-statements. Partners are sensitive to each other's moods. The faster you recover from a fight with your partner, the faster he will recover.[7]

Provide Distractions

Another way to help your partner calm down after a conflict may be to provide a distraction, such as suggesting you and he take a walk together or go to a store together to pick up a household item. Watching a movie or playing a game together are other distractions that can restore your partner's equanimity more quickly than sitting alone in a room.

These techniques can help an avoidant partner feel safe and secure during conflicts and can ensure that you retain your emotional connection with each other.

16

DANCE THE WALTZ
OF INTIMACY

It's one thing to learn how to help your partner manage her anxiety level during conflicts, but it's another to use these "partner buffering" techniques in the midst of one. In this chapter you will learn how to put buffering techniques to work, disentangle yourself from the stepcouple shuffle, restore harmony quickly, and dance the waltz of intimacy.

Both Kevin and Julia had several opportunities to develop these new skills. They had several fights about the way Julia felt Kevin treated her. In particular, she was jealous of his immediate response when his ex-wife asked him to fix something, such as a leaky faucet, in her home. He would drop everything and get to her house as fast as possible. When Julia asked him to repair something around their home, he claimed he was too tired to do it at that moment and procrastinated for days or weeks until he got around to it. Julia felt she was last on Kevin's list of priorities.

Kevin felt he had several reasons to jump at the opportunity to help his ex-wife. Primarily, he relished spending additional time with Matt and wanted to make sure his son was comfortable in his home. Also, Kevin derived satisfaction from knowing he was handy around the home and was saving his ex-wife from spending money on a plumber. He didn't have any romantic feelings for his ex-wife, so Julia's jealousy didn't make any sense to him. He didn't understand—and therefore couldn't explain to Julia—why it took him so long to fix things in their home.

While Julia understood and accepted Kevin's logic for helping his ex-wife, she believed actions speak louder than words. She concluded that Kevin's behavior truly indicated that he cared more about taking care of his ex-wife's needs than hers. Her jealousy grew stronger.

144

PUT BUFFERING TECHNIQUES TO WORK

Before Julia learned about partner buffering techniques, she exacerbated Kevin's insecurities by repeatedly and shrilly asking Kevin to delay going to his ex-wife's home to make repairs. She kept pushing him to acknowledge how she felt. Kevin grew more and more frustrated each time Julia repeated her request. He didn't like being controlled and became angry that Julia wanted to dictate when he should make repairs. He accused her of making a big deal out of nothing and called her controlling as well as crazy for believing he cared more about pleasing his ex-wife than her. You may agree with Kevin that Julia was making a mountain out of a molehill. His angry response, however, scared her to the point that she hesitated to bring up other topics that might cause Kevin to react defensively and decide to leave her.

After Kevin learned about partner buffering techniques, he realized he could alleviate Julia's insecurities by accepting her feelings as real even though they did not seem rational to him. He told her it was difficult for him to understand why she was feeling jealous but that she had nothing to worry about and he loved her very much. These reassuring statements helped Julia see her jealousy was unfounded.

Julia also worked diligently to improve their relationship by using buffering techniques for avoidant partners. She began sensitive conversations by telling Kevin how much she loved him. When she got to her request, she kept her voice neutral so he wouldn't get scared she was going to abandon him. On her first few attempts, he didn't notice the change in her tone of voice. He quickly became defensive and said, "You're yelling at me. I can never do anything right; I can never make you happy." Julia reassured him by saying, "I haven't raised my voice and I'm not criticizing you. I love you. Please be open to hear what I am saying to you."

Julia realized that if she wanted to have a true conversation with Kevin, she needed to let him express his feelings without correcting him. While she did not necessarily agree with his feelings, she had to respect his right to them and listen to him express them. As he got more in touch with his feelings, he was better able to express them.

Rather than explain her rationale multiple times, Julia made her request once. She realized that Kevin understood it the first time and just needed time to decide whether he was going to agree to change his behavior. She ended her statement by expressing appreciation to him for listening to her and taking her request into consideration. She also expressed confidence in his abilities to be flexible and accommodating.

Over time, Kevin was able to put himself in Julia's shoes and realized that if he were Julia, he too would resent waiting for repairs to be made in their home while he responded immediately to his ex-wife's requests. He promised to make repairs more quickly at home to prevent Julia from feeling her needs did not matter to him. He also told her he would consult with her before committing to fixing something at his ex-wife's home. And, most important, he followed through with this promise. Julia viewed this change of behavior as an indication that her happiness mattered to him. Kevin felt it was a small price to pay to ask her when she wanted him to go.

During conflicts, Kevin and Julia incorporated many of the buffering techniques described in the previous chapters, which improved their communication. In addition to relating to each other more openly and remaining emotionally connected, they helped each other become more secure.

Julia and Kevin are not unique. Partners can increase each other's security by becoming aware of their impact on each other during conflicts and then by following the buffering suggestions, which will help them become more gentle and forgiving. Researchers recently demonstrated this by examining the change in 32 distressed couples who each received 20 sessions of emotionally focused therapy (EFT).[1] Developed by Dr. Sue Johnson, this highly effective form of therapy focuses primarily on repairing attachment bonds by helping couples identify their attachment fears and then share these feelings in ways that pull them closer together.[2] (You can expedite the process of learning about and employing buffering techniques by going to a mental health professional trained in EFT.)

The couples who were selected to participate in the research study were unhappy in their relationships and had grown emotionally disconnected.[3] At the beginning of the study, they were given a list of questions to assess their attachment styles; everyone in the study was rated as either anxious or avoidant. Each couple then received 20 sessions of EFT to build greater trust, interdependence, and feelings of safety and security with each other. Afterward, they were asked to reevaluate themselves and their partners. Their responses were quite different from their initial assessments. They felt more emotionally available to, responsive to, and engaged with each other. They felt securely attached. In a follow-up two years later, these couples still saw their bond as secure and loving.

Partners can also help each other build resilience to stress. As we discussed in chapter 7, one study found differences in brain activity when subjects were threatened by an electric shock while holding their partner's hand, that of a stranger, or no hand at all.[4] The researchers found that there was significantly less brain activity when subjects held their partner's hand and concluded that a loving touch can protect us from the effects of stress. In a similar study by Dr. Johnson, she and her colleagues wanted to determine whether the quality of an intimate relationship affected brain activity.[5] They selected 24 unhappily married couples to participate in the study. Initially, holding a husband's hand did not buffer an unhappily married wife from the dread or pain of an electric shock, but after approximately 20 sessions of EFT couples therapy, it did. These studies underscore that we should not underestimate the importance of feeling secure with our partners.

LEARN THE WALTZ OF INTIMACY

By using the suggestions in this chapter and the preceding ones or by attending EFT sessions, you can become more secure and help your partner boost his or her security level as well. This will help disentangle you from the stepcouple shuffle during conflicts. Once this is accomplished, you will be able to learn new steps to communicate more effectively with each other when dealing with the most common stepfamily challenges. You will learn how to dance the "waltz of intimacy."

It's important to know the steps of the waltz of intimacy, since no one escapes the vagaries of life without some hardship. At one time or another, all stepcouples face challenges, such as the illness of a family member, the loss of a job with its resulting financial constraints, the irrational behavior of an ex-partner, or the social, behavioral, or academic problems of a child. These problems are more difficult to handle for stepcouples in which both partners are insecure than they are for those stepcouples in which one or both partners are secure.

While insecure partners end up doing the stepcouple shuffle so often that their emotional bonds fray, secure partners dance in unison during disagreements. They aren't beset with fear that their partners will reject them just because they hold differing opinions. They trust that their partner's love for them is constant and they don't push or pull each other.

Secure partners can stay focused on resolving the issue at hand without hurt or angry feelings getting in the way. They find it easier to compromise and are quick to forgive each other. Harmony is restored more quickly. They "dance" the waltz of intimacy.

Here are a few important differences between the ways secure and insecure partners communicate during conflicts:

- Secure partners remain calm throughout emotional discussions, which helps their partners to also remain calm. Insecure partners get upset, which intensifies their partner's distress.
- Secure partners respect each other during conflicts, while insecure ones hurt each other by lashing out in anger or withdrawing.
- During conflict, secure partners consider each other's feelings as much as their own. Hurt and angry feelings overwhelm insecure partners, and they lose sight of their partner's feelings.
- Secure partners trust that their partners love them, and during conflicts they are not concerned that they will be abandoned. During conflicts, insecure partners worry that their partners will reject them, and they dwell on these fears after the conflict is over.
- Secure partners clearly share their needs, while insecure ones passively or aggressively express theirs.
- During a conflict, secure partners protect each other's self-esteem by complaining about a partner's particular behavior rather than criticizing and undermining the other person's identity. Insecure partners can damage each other's self-esteem by being contemptuous during conflicts.
- Secure partners admit their mistakes and apologize for them. Insecure partners react defensively and justify their actions.
- Secure partners are quick to forgive, while insecure partners hold grudges for some time.

- Secure partners are comfortable telling their family and friends how much they love their partners. Insecure partners are uncomfortable sharing these loving feelings about partners with others.

In the next and last section of the book, I am going to illustrate how secure partners dance the waltz of intimacy when confronted with some common stepfamily problems. This will give you ideas for securely handling any problems you may encounter in the future while strengthening your emotional connection with each other.

Step 3

ADDRESS YOUR SPECIFIC STEPCOUPLE CHALLENGES

17

MANAGE INSIDER/
OUTSIDER ISSUES

Insider/outsider issues—problems created when one partner is excluded from the inner family circle—are very common for stepcouples. Despite your best intentions, have you found that one or more family members shut you out? They may not talk to you, make eye contact, or recognize anything you say or do, even when they are with you for long stretches of time. This is very hurtful.

You may think that the more secure you are, the less pain you will experience when excluded from a group conversation, decision, or activity. The truth is, we are all sensitive to even the slightest exclusion. Professor Kip Williams has studied ostracism (being ignored or shunned by others) and found that it doesn't take long for subjects to react to isolation from a group.[1] He stumbled upon this area of research while walking his dog in the park. He was hit by a Frisbee and tossed it back to one of the two guys who were playing with it. For a couple of minutes they included him in their game, and then suddenly excluded him. He was surprised by the sadness, anger, and embarrassment he felt when he was left out of the game.

Williams realized he could study ostracism and social exclusion by adapting his Frisbee experience in a laboratory setting. In one study he developed a computer game he named Cyberball.[2] The subjects chose an animated character to represent them and then played a game in which they tossed a ball back and forth with two other avatars. Though the subjects believed that the other avatars in the game were other participants in the study, in actuality, the computer was selecting which avatar to toss the ball to. At first it tossed the ball equally to each avatar, but after a few minutes, it completely excluded the subject's avatar from the game. It took only 20 seconds of being shunned from this game before research participants felt bad. If it takes only a few moments of being ignored by animated characters in a computer game to feel bad, imagine how hurt we feel when ignored by family members for long stretches of time!

Williams then hooked subjects up to an MRI while playing Cyberball and found that every participant reacted to the pain of ostracism in the area of the brain where we feel physical pain.[3] Most important, he found that we all react to the pain of ostracism equally, regardless of individual differences in toughness or sensitivity. What's more, an emotional wound may be more difficult to heal than a physical one. Baumeister and Leary contend that two of our most basic needs—belonging and self-esteem—are threatened when we are excluded from a group.[4] This throws us emotionally off-kilter, and it can affect everything from empathy to intelligent thought.

I was quite relieved after reading these studies, because along with feeling hurt when I was ignored or excluded in the past, I also felt shame. I thought I was overreacting to experiences that someone who was more secure than I may not have even noticed. Once, for example, one of my husband's relatives left a Happy New Year message for him on our answering machine without mentioning me. I felt upset that I was not included in this message while at the same time thinking I was being too sensitive and immature. These studies of ostracism made me realize that my hurt feelings after being slighted were completely normal.

Similar to me, many stepmothers with whom I worked expressed feelings of shame when their stepchildren wouldn't play with them, eat their food, or talk to them. By the way, this happens frequently. In my survey, 45 percent of respondents indicated that they either frequently or occasionally dealt with an emotionally distant stepchild, while another 42 percent dealt with stepchildren whose loyalty to their biological parents prevented them from getting close. Many of these survey participants said they felt bad that a child's behavior could elicit such strong negative reactions. They believed they needed to grow thicker skins. As a result of Williams's studies, now we know that thick skin doesn't matter and that anyone would react to rejection with pain.[5]

Now it is true that we differ in how we manage emotional pain. Socially anxious participants took longer to recover from playing Cyberball than subjects who had less social anxiety.[6] While it took 45 minutes for the effects of ostracism to completely dissipate for subjects with low anxiety, the effects lingered for those with social anxiety, who reported perceiving the world in a more threatening manner.

ATTACHMENT STYLE AND INSIDER/OUTSIDER ISSUES

The more secure we are, the more quickly we bounce back from ostracism. As I've grown more secure in my marriage over the years, I've noticed a difference in my response when I feel like an outsider in my family. In the past, I had an avoidant reaction. I would not admit I was hurt. Instead I would remain silent and develop a grudge against the person who had hurt me. Recently I behaved very differently. My husband told me about a conversation he had with my pregnant stepdaughter. She told him about a vaccine that family and friends could take to protect newborns against whooping cough. Although she did not directly ask him to get vaccinated, he told me he would get the vaccine at the hospital where he worked. I then asked, "What about me?" He explained it wasn't absolutely necessary for me to be vaccinated because there hasn't been a case of whooping cough on the East Coast for many years.

I was taken aback by his response and was hurt that he didn't think it was equally important for me to get vaccinated. Was he suggesting that a stepgrandparent isn't as close a family member as a biological one? I decided to give myself a little time to think about what specifically was bothering me before sharing my feelings with him. I waited until the following evening and told him that his reaction to my question about the vaccine made me feel like an outsider in our family. I explained that he quickly made plans to get vaccinated but did not consider my need to get one. I said this calmly and succinctly. I didn't build a case against him by providing examples of other times I did not feel included in family events. When I kept my message short, my husband was able to listen to me without getting defensive. He said he understood why I came to the conclusion I had and apologized for hurting me. He added that while he thought of us a team, he realized he didn't always act as my teammate. He then called a friend who is a doctor and asked him to order a vaccine for me.

Based on the ostracism research, it's important to note that no matter my attachment style, I was going to be hurt when my husband did not consider my need to get the vaccine. However, my level of security did really affect the way I dealt with feeling hurt. By reacting in a secure manner, I was able to directly tell my husband what was bothering me, was willing to accept his apology, and could let go of the hurt pretty quickly. I danced the waltz of intimacy. If I'd had an avoidant reaction, I would have compounded my feeling like an outsider by actively choosing to be one. I might have refused to go with my husband to meet my newborn grandchild, citing the possibility I might get her sick. As you might imagine, this passive-aggressive response would have caused a lot of problems between my husband and me. What a relief that my secure reaction avoided this tension!

How we bounce back from conflicts doesn't just depend on our security level, it also depends upon our partners' security level. The more secure they are, the better they will respond to and help us deal with pain when we are rejected. While it's impossible to predict when an insider/outsider issue will occur, awareness of its potential can nip its harmful effects in the bud. Here is an example of the difference between secure and insecure reactions that two husbands, Brad and Carlos, had after their wives felt like outsiders in church.

Brad's wife, Chloe, described her experience in this way:

I was at church with Brad, my stepson, and my mother-in-law when Brad's ex-wife walked in. She sat down right between my mother-in-law and my husband. She tried to talk to Brad all during the service; he kept telling her to keep quiet. When the service was over, she gave my mother-in-law a big hug goodbye and completely ignored me. Even though I knew her behavior was rude, ridiculous, and inappropriate, I still felt like an intruder in my family. How dare she waltz in to church and act like she is still married to my husband when she was the one who walked out on him!

Brad was very angry about his ex-wife's behavior. He resented that her violation of his space ruined his experience at church, and he told Chloe how frustrated he was that he had no power to control her behavior or prevent it from happening again. He went as far as to say he didn't want to attend any more church services. As he vented to Chloe, he hoped she would soothe his feelings. However, he did not ask how Chloe felt about his ex-wife's behavior. She was hurt by his seeming lack of concern for her feelings and concluded that she could not trust him to consider her needs and feelings in awkward situations. Can you guess Brad's emotional style? (Brad is anxious.)

Believe it or not, Chloe's experience at church is not that uncommon. Something similar happened to an African American stepmother, Tanya, who was married to a Caucasian husband, Carlos. They attended a church whose members were mostly white. During one Sunday service, Tanya's stepson was seated between them, when Carlos's ex-wife sat down between him and his son. Carlos was uncomfortable with this seating arrangement but did not want to cause a scene by changing seats. So he grabbed Tanya's hand and held it for the entire church service. He was sensitive to Tanya's feeling that she did not fully fit in with the congregants and wanted to rectify the isolation he knew she was feeling because of his ex-wife's behavior. Can you guess Carlos's emotional style? (Carlos is secure.)

The difference between the ways Brad and Carlos handled these situations may seem minor, yet it made a big difference in Chloe and Tanya's feelings of safety and security. Brad took an approach step to start the stepcouple shuffle, hoping that when he reached out to Chloe, she would help him feel better. His reaction exacerbated Chloe's feeling like an outsider in her family, and she now felt unsafe with Brad. Tanya was as disturbed as Chloe by the behavior of Carlos's ex-wife, but he soothed her distress by holding her hand. This small gesture went a long way in helping Tanya feel safe and secure in their relationship. Carlos never lost sight of Tanya's feelings and helped her remain emotionally connected with him. He danced the waltz of intimacy.

We can't prevent others from excluding our partners; however, we can mitigate our partners' hurt by recognizing ostracism as it occurs and dealing with it as quickly as possible. Just as it doesn't take much for others to hurt our partners, it doesn't take much to help them heal from emotional injury. One more example to highlight this pertains to how secure and insecure husbands handled their wives' distress after they and their children did not receive any holiday gifts from their new in-laws.

Holidays are supposedly occasions when we celebrate family and love, but ironically, they are times when outsider injuries frequently take place. Two newly remarried couples shared similar experiences with very different outcomes. The first stepcouple, Iris and Justin (both with two children from prior relationships), were invited to Justin's parents' home to celebrate Christmas. They brought gifts for everyone in the family. As everyone's gifts were handed out, it became clear that Justin's family had not bought any presents for Iris and her children. She was both embarrassed and hurt by this and concluded it was a statement about their unwillingness to include her and her children in their family.

Once they got home, Iris told Justin she was hurt by his family's omission and was particularly upset for her children. Justin explained to Iris that his family's insensitivity was typical, so she shouldn't take it personally. Iris felt criticized by this remark, since she was taking it personally. She then felt worse when Justin added that it shouldn't matter to her children that his family didn't give them gifts because they received lots of other ones. While true, this was beside the point for Iris. She wanted Justin to acknowledge that as a parent, he understood her desire to protect her children from unnecessary pain. All she wanted him to say was "I'm so sorry my family hurt you and your children. What an embarrassing and painful situation for you to be in!"

In fact, Justin did feel bad for Iris and her children but did not know what to say or do. He felt paralyzed and ineffectual. Based on prior experiences with his family, he knew that they wouldn't listen to him if he asked them to be more considerate to Iris and her children. His discomfort with talking to them overshadowed his ability to identify with and acknowledge Iris's feelings. He wished the problems would just disappear and hoped that telling her she shouldn't feel bad about his family's oversight would help her let go of the hurt. Peace and harmony between them would then be restored. He took the avoidant second step of the stepcouple shuffle. Can you guess his emotional style? (Justin is avoidant.)

The problem is, Justin's tactic of telling Iris she shouldn't feel a certain way never works. Not only doesn't it change her feelings, it makes her feel worse. She also feels misunderstood. Justin had no idea that Iris felt judged by him and would be less willing to share her feelings with him in the future. He had no idea his comment would cause her to grow more reserved and distant. Even though this incident is minor compared to more major traumas in life, it harmed their relationship. In contrast, a secure reaction from another husband in a similar experience made a big difference to his wife—and to their relationship.

Lori and Elijah, the other newly remarried couple (each of whom had one child from a prior relationship), spent their first Christmas with Elijah's parents. No one in Elijah's family bought Lori or her daughter a gift. Elijah noticed this as others were unwrapping their presents and whispered to Lori, asking if she wanted him to mention this to his family. Lori shook her head no. As they were heading to their car to go home, Elijah grabbed Lori and gave her a big hug. He told her he was so sorry his family behaved so poorly and then asked her what she wanted him to do. Did she want him to talk to his parents or siblings? Lori wasn't sure that would help. Elijah then told her about a time as a teenager he felt like an outsider when visiting his friend. His friend's mother called everyone to dinner but told him to stay in his friend's bedroom until the meal was finished. After dinner, she called up to him and asked if he wanted to have dessert with them. He said he was mortified to be excluded and never went back to that friend's house. He could understand if Lori decided she didn't want to visit his family again. By sharing this experience, Elijah demonstrated to Lori that he knew how bad she felt, and this eased her pain. He danced the waltz of intimacy.

Elijah put himself in Lori's shoes and knew she was hurt by his family's omission. He wanted to help her and asked her permission to talk to his parents about their insensitive behavior toward Lori and her daughter. He was willing to accept that his relationship with them might be strained after he talked to them. The next day he asked his parents why they didn't bother to get Lori or her daughter a present. They said they didn't think they had to. Elijah said Lori and her daughter were his family now. He loved them very much and would appreciate it if his parents accepted them. To demonstrate their approval, he would appreciate if, in the future, they would give them holiday presents. His parents didn't object but didn't apologize for their oversight either. Not trusting their ability to follow through with his request, he made a note that he would remind them to get Lori and her daughter presents on their birthdays and the following Christmas.

STRATEGIES TO HANDLE
INSIDER/OUTSIDER ISSUES

There are several effective ways to handle insider/outsider issues to support your partner and your relationship. We'll explore these below.

Respond Immediately

As we saw with Elijah, secure partners react immediately when they notice that a family member (or someone else) is excluding their partner. Even though they may not be able to prevent this from happening again, they understand that they can soothe their partner's distress by acknowledging the slight. They know that feeling understood by another person is a powerful antidote to suffering, whereas feeling that one's hurt is ignored or deemed inconsequential only exacerbates the pain.

Express sympathy to your partner each time she is feeling like an outsider. This can prevent your partner's hurt from building up and damaging her trust in you. Julia often felt like an outsider with Kevin and his son. Kevin did not realize he was adding to her pain each time he did not tell his son to answer her questions. He was fortunate that he hadn't experienced what it feels like to be an outsider, and he didn't understand how hurt Julia felt to be left out of his inner circle. Easing her pain would have been simple: all he needed to say to her was "I'm so sorry Matt didn't answer your question. I know it doesn't feel good to be ignored." She would have perceived this statement as an acknowledgment of, and an attempt to reduce, her pain. This would have been the difference between strengthening and weakening their emotional connection.

Encourage Separate Activities

Secure partners encourage family members to get to know their partners independently. Because Kevin was so insecure about his son's love, he felt uncomfortable encouraging Julia to forge her own relationship with Matt by spending time doing separate activities. If he had been more secure, he might have suggested that Julia take Matt to the movies or shopping on her own. He might have found excuses to leave their home so Julia and Matt could play a board or video game together. His insecurity was preventing them all from getting to their common goal of family harmony.

Plan for the Future

Insider/outsider issues often diminish over time as family members adjust to the permanence of their relationship, but they do not disappear entirely for everyone. Surprisingly, these issues can resurface for some after many years together, in particular when a partner requires medical care. Even if they had an excellent relationship beforehand, a stepparent and adult stepchildren are likely to have differences of opinion regarding treatment options and financial decisions for the ill partner/parent. Some researchers studied a small sample of women who, later in life, had remarried men with adult children.[7] These women were in their midsixties, married on average for 17 years, and cared for husbands with Alzheimer's disease or another form of dementia.

The research participants were asked to complete questionnaires about their responsibilities as caregivers, their social networks, and their levels of depression. They were also asked about the amount of disagreement they experienced with family and stepfamily members regarding decisions for their husbands' medical care. Most of the women reported that their adult stepchildren rejected their remarriage and had minimal involvement in taking care of their fathers. Two-thirds of the women stated that their stepchildren did not provide any help for their fathers' care. Instead they offered unwanted advice, interfered, or meddled with the women's decisions. Oftentimes they made hurtful, inconsiderate, and critical comments about their stepmothers' care, and they failed to follow through with their promises to help. The women were forced to rely on friends and neighbors for comfort from their burdens and to ease their sense of isolation.

The results of this study are upsetting. However, secure partners will understand that despite having a warm and loving relationship with their stepchildren that spans several decades, their relationship may change once their partner falls ill. They can plan in advance by talking to their partners in a calm, rational way about what they should do in the event that this happens.

Insider/outsider issues can also surface when older stepparents need care from their adult stepchildren. You might expect that after years of care from stepparents, stepchildren would reciprocate when their stepparents need help. However, adult stepchildren may not see this as their responsibility if they do not consider a stepparent a part of their family.

Researchers at the Pew Research Center found that stepfamilies don't have as strong a sense of kinship as traditional ones, and consequently members don't feel as obligated to help those who are not blood-related.[8] They asked adult subjects to rank their level of obligation to different family members and close friends who needed financial assistance or help taking care of themselves. Eighty-five percent of respondents said they would help their biological parents, while only 56 percent felt obligated to help a stepparent. Sixty-four percent of the participants said they would be willing to help a biological sibling in serious trouble, while only 42 percent felt obligated to assist a step- or half-sibling. Based on these results, it appears that blood does run thicker than water.

Although these are sobering and cautionary results, they can serve as a reminder of the importance of responding to challenges in a secure manner. Given the chance that your stepchildren may not be a source of support later in life, you can strengthen your friendships now in order to have a larger support network to draw upon for help when you get older, save money for retirement, and, if possible, invest in a long-term-care insurance policy. As with any regenerated family issue, insider/outsider issues are easier to deal with the more secure you and your partner are. Now let's turn our attention to securely handling a partner's jealousy.

18

TAME YOUR PARTNER'S
GREEN-EYED MONSTER

Jealousy is an emotion everyone experiences at some point, and it can range from mild to extreme. In small doses, jealousy can be positive for a relationship because it can prevent partners from taking each other for granted. When it is intense or irrational, though, it can cause a lot of damage. For many stepcouples, it is quite common for jealousy to rear its ugly head.

At the core of jealousy is fear of loss. Many of the conflicts stepcouples experience stem from one partner believing that someone or something has the power to cause the other partner to end their relationship. Sometimes a real threat triggers an insecure partner's jealousy, while at other times it stems solely from one's imagination. Whether real or imagined, once activated, a threat is seen as absolute proof of impending abandonment. The following statements highlight the thoughts of insecure partners:

> *I am not worthy of my partner's love. I am not good enough. I am not pretty/ handsome/intelligent/warm/funny/sexy/loving/fill-in-the-blank enough for him/her.*

> *My partner doesn't love me and would rather be with his/her ex or someone new. My partner can decide to leave me at any time.*

WHAT TRIGGERS JEALOUSY?

Many of my clients expressed a belief that their partners' exes wanted to resume a relationship with their partners. Or they feared their partners were still in love with their exes who left them for someone else. If given the opportunity, their partners would return to the ex. My clients doubted they could compete with the exes to win their partners' affection. Jealous feelings soon followed.

Some of my clients were upset that they were not their partner's first love. They had a difficult time accepting that their partners experienced many firsts, including some momentous occasions, such as a wedding or the birth of children, with someone else. Their destiny as the second, third, or even fourth love was a bitter pill for them to swallow.

It is not just a partner's past that can trigger jealousy. Some of my clients had been betrayed by a former partner and concluded that it was only a matter of time before they would be hurt again. No matter how loyal and faithful their current partner was, they were convinced that eventually this relationship also would end.

Not all family members sever their relationships with their relative's partner just because that relationship ends. Jealous feelings also can be triggered if a partner's parents or other relatives maintain a friendship with their former daughter- or son-in-law. One stepmother, Nora, became jealous when her husband's uncle sat next to and chatted with his ex-wife at her stepdaughter's dance recitals and ignored Nora. He may not have been conscious of the message he was sending her, but Nora concluded he cared only for her predecessor and felt jealous and upset that he did not make an effort to be friendly to her.

These examples may not seem egregious enough to merit intense feelings of jealousy, but that's just the point. It doesn't take a significant transgression, such as an emotional or physical betrayal, to trigger jealousy. It can be brought on by behaviors that one partner views as completely innocent while the other one distinguishes them as potentially harmful to their relationship.

Can you relate to any of these common ways jealousy is triggered in a stepcouple relationship?

- Your partner is more generous to her children than to you.
- Your partner allows her children, in your presence, to reminisce about vacations taken with her ex without trying to change the topic to one that includes you. You feel excluded from the conversation and are jealous you were not part of this experience.

- Your in-laws still have photos of your partner and her ex prominently displayed in their home. Constant reminders of your partner's past make you uncomfortable.
- Your partner maintains connections with her former in-laws on Facebook.
- Your partner talks a lot about past experiences she had with her ex.
- Your partner is more worried about pleasing her ex-partner than you.
- Your partner readjusts plans with you to fulfill the requests of her ex.
- Your partner spends more time, money, or energy on her ex-partner than you.
- Your partner speaks to or texts her ex-partner about subjects other than their children.
- Your partner lies about the amount of time she spends with her ex-partner.
- You've caught your partner texting her ex or another person unnecessarily.
- Your partner hides her phone from you so you can't scroll through her text messages.
- Your partner takes phone calls in private.
- Your partner comes home late without calling and then avoids explaining what she was doing.
- Your partner evades answering your questions.
- Your partner is more attentive to others than to you. You feel taken for granted.
- Your partner is flirtatious with others in your presence.
- Your partner attends parties without you.

HOW TO ASSUAGE AND HANDLE JEALOUSY

Many of the situations listed above come with the territory of stepcouple relationships. What can you do, however, if you or your partner experience one or more of them?

Empathize

First and foremost, you want to ease each other's concerns. Secure partners try to put themselves in their partners' shoes and empathize with the pain they are experiencing. They don't dig in their heels and defend their behaviors when their partners admit to jealousy. They realize that underlying their partner's jealousy lies a fear about the stability of their relationship and a need to be reassured that it is on solid footing.

Secure partners don't jump to conclusions about what would alleviate their partners' jealousy. They understand that their partners may not want them to totally give up the particular activity that piques the jealousy. For example, if you are jealous of the generosity your partner bestows upon her children, I bet you don't want her to stop being generous to them because it's probably a quality you love and respect. You just want your partner to treat you equally. If you are jealous of the amount of contact your partner has with her ex, you understand all contact can't be eliminated, but you just want your partner to enforce stricter boundaries to protect your relationship. Drastic changes are not always needed to assuage a partner's jealousy.

In other instances, a bigger behavioral change may be necessary to alleviate a partner's jealousy. Secure partners ask their partners what it would take to reduce their jealousy and may commit to changing this behavior, at least temporarily. If this isn't possible or they are unable or unwilling to comply with what their partner asks them to do, they find a compromise that satisfies both of them. A small gesture may go a long way in relieving a partner's insecurity.

Don't Minimize Your Partner's Concern

It's not just a particular behavior that can trigger a partner's jealousy. When a partner reveals jealous feelings, your reaction to that disclosure really matters. You can either exacerbate or soothe your partner's insecurities by reacting agreeably or with resistance.

After Julia told Kevin she was jealous that he jumped to help his wife but did not make a repair in their home, initially he did not react well. In the heat of the moment, he called her controlling and crazy. He responded defensively because he felt his autonomy was being threatened. While this explains his behavior, it does not excuse it. As stated previously, name-calling damages a partner's self-esteem and weakens a couple's emotional connection with each other. Secure partners understand that contempt is the most destructive element of communication and do not resort to using it during conflicts. Make sure you and your partner

- do not belittle, humiliate, shame, or make fun of each other for having jealous feelings,
- do not suggest either of you is crazy, and
- do not react defensively or get annoyed that your partner could even consider that you have romantic feelings toward a former partner or by another behavior that upsets your partner.

After Kevin learned about partner buffering techniques, he reacted more sensitively when Julia expressed jealous feelings. He reassured her that he loved her very much, which really helped Julia feel more secure.

Be Open and Transparent

Julia directly told Kevin which of his behaviors was making her jealous. Some partners are not as comfortable being so specific. They are ashamed to admit to jealousy since our culture stigmatizes those who experience it. Instead they may act out their jealousy in unhealthy ways by constantly monitoring their partner's whereabouts, by surreptitiously checking their phone or computer history, or by trying to limit contact with their family or friends. If your partner engages in these tactics, you may decide to protect your independence and privacy by being secretive or omitting details of conversations you have with others. While your instincts to protect your autonomy are completely natural, hiding or withholding information from your partner only increases her jealous feelings.

Secure partners strive to be as open as possible with partners, knowing it will help them feel more secure. If you omit details of plans or withhold information from your partner because you know it would cause a fight, consider that it's better to face potential conflict sooner rather than later. Try to become more self-disclosing. This will help rebuild your partner's trust. If your partner wants to know the content of your texts and emails with ex-partners or others, provide this information. Leave your phone unlocked or provide your partner with your password to it and your computer. Rather than think of this as supervision, view it as a choice you are making to help your partner heal. While this may seem like a violation of your privacy, for a short period of time, it can help your partner overcome jealousy. Your partner won't be interested in checking up on you when she feels secure.

Don't Overshare

While some partners' jealousy is assuaged when they know all details, others become jealous when they receive too much information from partners, as was the case with one client after her husband kept pointing out attractive women on the street. He would say, "Isn't she attractive?" When she told him this statement made her uncomfortable, he would dismiss her feelings by saying, "It's silly for you to get jealous of someone I don't know and am not getting involved with." At first he didn't see that by oversharing, he was fueling his wife's jealousy. He finally understood its effect when she asked him what he intended to communicate by sharing this information. What was his message, and how did he want her to respond? He thought about it and recognized he was treating her like one of his male buddies, and he couldn't expect her to respond to his comments like one. Unintentionally, his disclosure was a form of cruelty.

There are many other ways to overshare. If you have tendencies to do this, ask your partner what information he or she wants to be told about and restrict yourself to sharing only that.

Set Boundaries with Others Outside Your Relationship

Additionally, don't overshare intimate details of your relationship with your parents, children, or ex-partners. Infidelity is not just a physical act; it can be just as painful when you become too friendly or too close with someone outside of your relationship.

Be Truthful

It goes without saying that you need to do your best to be truthful at all times. Even small white lies fuel an anxious partner's jealousy.

If caught in one, you will lose your partner's trust, and her insecurities will increase.

Give Extra Doses of Love

Last but not least, try to show your partner extra love when she is jealous. This is a time to be most generous with your affection.

If none of these suggestions ease your partner's jealousy, consider going to couples counseling together. In a neutral setting, a mental health practitioner may help the two of you de-escalate the tension that is tearing apart your relationship.

19

CONSTRUCT HEALTHY
BOUNDARIES

Let's shift our attention to another common problem stepcouples experience—boundary violations—and examine how secure partners deal with them. First, let's define what a boundary is. A boundary is an invisible, self-determined line that protects us in various ways from absorbing others' unhealthy behaviors, attitudes, or emotions. Boundaries are very important in helping to keep us emotionally and physically safe. Additionally, they

- help us stand up for ourselves,
- protect our bodies from being touched without our consent,
- prevent our thoughts and feelings from being manipulated by others,
- ensure our material possessions are kept safe, unavailable to others without our permission,
- prevent our time and energy from being exhausted by others' unreasonable demands,
- give us the ability to say no to unreasonable requests, and
- help us to accept hearing no from others without damaging our self-esteem.

Each of our boundaries is unique, created by a combination of our personal preferences, our family and cultural backgrounds, and our security levels. Some of us develop healthy boundaries, while others form rigid or porous ones. Some of us can maintain healthy boundaries in certain realms, such as at work, yet have porous ones in others.

At one end of the spectrum lie rigid boundaries. They keep others at an emotional distance, make it difficult to ask others for help, and restrict disclosure of personal information. Those who have rigid boundaries can be lonely. Sound familiar? These characteristics are similar to those of people with avoidant tendencies. However, not everyone who has rigid boundaries is avoidant. Other factors, such as family and cultural influences, also play a role.

Porous boundaries lie at the other end of the spectrum. People with porous boundaries share characteristics similar to those who have anxious tendencies. (Again, not everyone with porous boundaries is anxious.) Those with porous boundaries are extremely sensitive to other people's emotions, thoughts, and behavior. They find it difficult to say no to others' requests and often end up feeling disrespected or taken advantage of when they do not receive adequate appreciation for their efforts. They struggle to make decisions and depend on others to help make them. When criticized by others, albeit constructively, they react defensively and their self-esteem plummets. They also tend to overshare personal information.

IDENTIFYING BOUNDARIES

Many of us are unaware of the concept of boundaries and have never considered what type we have. We haven't had the need. We grow up with certain family customs, such as keeping bedroom doors open or closed, and accept them as the norm without identifying them as boundary choices. I hadn't realized what one of mine was—wanting family and friends to call before dropping by our apartment—until my husband casually mentioned his mother would "pop over" to visit us. I thought it was customary for everyone to call before going to someone's home, and I was surprised my mother-in-law didn't do this and that my husband didn't expect her to. It was only then that I realized that he and I had different boundaries.

Boundary differences between partners often become apparent and then problematic when stepcouples begin to live together. Oftentimes the stepparent believes she must adopt certain family customs to fit in despite feeling uncomfortable. For example, after living with her partner, Nate, for a couple of months, Kyla felt pressured to go out to lunch or dinner once a month with his children and his ex-wife. Nate and his ex-wife remained friendly after their divorce, and she suggested everyone to get together "for the sake of the children." Nate passed her request along to Kyla.

This request is not as unusual as you may think. A small percentage (approximately 10 percent) of former couples can be categorized as "perfect pals" who remain friendly after a breakup.[1] They keep in touch with each other's extended family members, ask the other for advice, and even spend holidays together. A new partner might be expected to accept and join this friendship. Some new partners may be open to this arrangement while others would object to it.

While Kyla got along with Nate's ex-wife, she felt a pit in her stomach when thinking about going out to dinner with her. This request extended beyond Kyla's comfort zone. She envisioned feeling like an outsider when Nate, his ex-wife, and their children reminisced about past experiences. She would be unable to participate in these conversations, and she'd feel lonely.

Kyla also disagreed with Nate's ex-wife and didn't think getting together was healthy for her stepchildren. Seeing their parents spend time together would give them false hope that their parents would reunite. While she understood children suffered when their parents continued to fight after a divorce, she did not see how Nate's children would benefit from getting together with everyone for a monthly meal. She believed that all they needed to lead happy, healthy lives was for the adults in the family to be civil, polite, and respectful to each other. Friendship wasn't a requirement. At first Kyla did not feel she was entitled to turn down this request. To prove she was a family team member, she felt she had to go along with it.

As long as you remain respectful and compassionate with your partner, you can say no to family requests that will harm you. After talking to some other stepmothers, Kyla realized she could not handle going to monthly dinners that included Nate's ex-wife. In a kind and considerate manner, she told Nate she wasn't willing to have dinner with her. Nate was actually relieved. He wasn't thrilled with the idea either but felt he had to pass his ex-wife's request along to Kyla. Nate and Kyla were lucky that this request did not cause problems between them. It just highlighted their boundary preferences.

What would you do in this situation? Would you feel obliged to agree to your partner's request for "the good of your stepchildren" or for your partner's benefit? Would you be able to say no? While it's important to be considerate of your partner's needs, if your boundary is going to be crossed by a request, it's important to be able to say no to a partner (or anyone else for that matter) and share this information in a manner that strengthens rather than weakens your emotional connection with each other.

RECOGNIZING BOUNDARY VIOLATIONS

You may be wondering how to identify your boundaries. Kyla had a physical symptom, a knot in the pit of her stomach, when she thought about dinner with Nate's ex-wife. She knew this stemmed from a feeling of dread rather than from a physical cause. You can identify your boundaries by paying attention to how you feel both emotionally and physically after a request is made or after you spend time with certain people. Ask yourself these two questions:

- Do you feel tired, get a headache, or have neck or stomach pain after spending time with certain people? Pay attention to any physical symptoms you develop. They can signal that your boundary is being violated.
- Do you feel resentful, frustrated, sad, or angry after spending time with certain people? Have they done something to upset you? These nagging feelings also may be giving you information about your boundaries.

When someone crosses one of your boundaries by invading your space without your permission or by making unreasonable demands of your time, for example, it is considered a boundary violation. Unfortunately, boundary violations are as common for stepcouples as insider/outsider issues. In fact, more than 80 percent of respondents to my survey experienced this in some way, shape, or form. This is not so surprising when you consider that modern technology makes it faster and easier for us to be contacted than ever before. We are more vulnerable to privacy invasion through daily emails, texts, and phone calls. Let's look at some of the more common ways others may violate your boundaries:

- Your partner's ex may enter your home or apartment without your consent.
- Your partner's ex may not abide by the custody agreement and drop off your stepchildren at his designated time, expecting you to be a last-minute babysitter.
- Your adult stepchildren may move back home without first consulting with you.
- Family members may barge into your space when you are getting dressed, using the bathroom, or taking a shower.
- Your stepchildren may borrow your clothes and personal items without permission. They may take money from your wallet without your consent.
- Your partner may share with his children or parents too much intimate information that you want kept confidential.
- Your phone or emails may be hacked.
- Another family member may force you to listen to loud music or TV, disregarding your need for serenity.
- You may be exposed to physical illnesses without any consideration for your health.
- You may be dragged into family problems that you have had nothing to do with.
- Family members may make demands on your time and be unwilling to take no for an answer.

How many, if any, of these boundary violations have you and your partner experienced?

HANDLING BOUNDARY VIOLATIONS

Many of the issues that stepcouples face can be classified as boundary violations. One of the most common ones relates to how much contact with an ex-partner is appropriate. One stepmother, Maya, complained that she had no idea what she agreed to when her stepchildren begged for a puppy and convinced her to split its care with their mother. She assumed that the dog would follow the same custody schedule as her stepchildren, living with her and her partner 50 percent of the time and spending the rest of the time at the biological mother's home. Imagine her surprise when, during her time with the dog, her partner's ex came to her home four times a day to walk it. Because they shared the dog, she saw her partner's ex much more than she did through splitting custody of her stepchildren!

As you well know by now, when both partners are insecure, the clash of their attachment styles weakens their emotional connection. Both Maya and her husband, Liam, were avoidant, and they tried to circumvent all conversations that had the potential for conflict. While Maya was bothered by the excessive interactions with Liam's ex-wife, she allowed them to continue for several weeks. Finally she gathered the courage to ask him to tell his ex-wife to stop coming to their home to walk the dog. Liam understood how annoying it was to have his ex-wife come to his home four times a day. In fact, he hid in the basement or bathroom when she came over. He told Maya he would talk to his ex-wife but never found the time. Because his ex-wife resorted to threats when she didn't get her way, he particularly hated confrontations with her. He was afraid she would threaten to keep his children from him if he asked her to stop dropping by.

Since Liam never asked his ex-wife to stop coming over to walk the dog, Maya believed she had two choices: accept the situation or leave. After several weeks of trying to accept the situation, she realized she could not tolerate it and told Liam she was planning to leave him. This spurred him to take action. He loved Maya and did not want their relationship to end. Liam talked to his ex-wife and told her he and Maya would take full responsibility for the pup while in their care. She was not welcome to come to their home to walk the dog.

If Maya were more secure, she would have spoken up more quickly and told Liam how uncomfortable she was seeing his ex-wife multiple times a day. When bringing this up, she could have remained calm and compassionate, sensitive to his avoidant tendencies, and said, "I know your ex-wife has no boundaries, and you tried and failed to implement them with her in the past. I know you feel hopeless that you will succeed now, but for me could you please try one more time? Please tell her she is no longer welcome to come to our home to walk the dog."

If Liam were more secure, he too would have behaved differently. He would have acknowledged Maya's feelings by telling her he understood her distress in seeing his ex-wife so frequently. This would demonstrate how much he cared for Maya and would build her confidence that she could depend upon him. After acknowledging Maya's feelings, Liam then could have had a conversation with his ex-wife setting guidelines for her to follow.

Stepcouples can have their space and privacy invaded in a myriad of other ways. One woman emailed or texted her ex-husband, Amir, several times each day and night, even when he did not have custody of his children. She shared anecdotes about the kids, asked his advice about cooking a dish, or gossiped about friends and neighbors. None of these correspondences was an emergency, yet Amir responded immediately, thinking this was the polite, respectful, and right thing to do. His behavior pattern continued from the time he separated from his ex-wife until he began to date and then moved in with Emma, who quickly became annoyed by these intrusions. She did not understand why he had to respond while having dinner, watching a movie, and, believe it or not, having sex. The moment Amir heard his phone ping, he would stop what he was doing and respond to any text or email, the majority of which were from his ex-wife.

Emma asked Amir to put his phone in another room when they were eating, watching a movie, or sleeping. He told Emma he would think about her request, but this was just a stalling tactic he often used rather than directly turning down her request. He did not want to disappoint Emma or fight with her, yet he was unwilling to be separated from his phone.

Because Emma was mildly anxious, she pushed Amir to change his behavior. Her requests grew more demanding until she could no longer tolerate who she was becoming: a nagging girlfriend. In desperation, she told Amir that based on his behavior, she didn't believe he truly loved her. In her mind, actions speak louder than words, and he wasn't expressing his love for her in a meaningful way. If Emma had been more secure, she would have remained calm when asking Amir to wait a few minutes before responding to emails, texts, and voice messages.

Below we'll see how Emma and Amir took steps to handle these boundary violations, and I'll introduce two other couples who used some other effective strategies.

Small Steps

Emma thought about breaking up with Amir. Before making such a drastic move, she suggested he talk to his friends about their phone usage and compare his behavior to theirs. She hoped he would realize that his relationship with his phone was unhealthy and was creating problems for them. Amir did talk to several friends about their phone usage and was surprised they did not keep their phones by their sides at all times. He finally understood why Emma believed his relationship with his phone was more important to him than his relationship with her. If he did not change his behavior, he was going to ruin their relationship.

Amir was not the only one to whom his ex-wife sent incessant messages. She constantly contacted their two sons when they were spending time with Amir and Emma. Both Amir and Emma objected to interruptions by her texts or phone calls during mealtimes and other activities. Yet they hadn't taken any action to rectify this behavior. Both were too scared to confront his ex-wife.

Even though Amir's ex-wife could be challenging to talk to, I was confident a conversation with her would not devolve into a battle. There was a secure way to handle this problem. I suggested they establish a new household policy to prevent inappropriate or excessive intrusions from entering their space at certain times. Everyone, including Amir's children, must abide by a new rule that stipulates no one will answer phone calls or respond to text messages during meals or during activities outside the home. Amir's sons would keep their phones in their bedrooms during meals and would wait until everyone was finished eating before speaking to or texting their mother. They would also leave their phones at home when they went to the movies or the park. Amir liked this idea and told his two young sons about the new rule. He was surprised that they readily agreed to this new policy.

Establish Healthy Boundaries

Amir then called his ex-wife and said something like this: "I want to let you know about a change we've made in our household. Up until now, we have allowed phone calls during lunch or dinner. They have been very intrusive, and from now on, we are going to let all calls go to voice mail. If you happen to call when we're eating, I will make sure the kids call you back right after the meal."

When talking to his ex-wife, Amir was careful he didn't blame Emma for these rule changes, so as not to make her out as the bad guy. He made it clear that it was a joint decision.

My House, My Rules

To ensure that their space remains sacred, some stepcouples will need to establish strict household rules. They may have to prevent ex-partners from entering their home and ask them to wait by the front door when picking up or dropping off their children. One stepmother, Natalya, noticed a trend. Her husband's ex-wife would spend more and more time in her home when dropping off her children. Natalya reached her limit when she found out her nanny prepared this woman lunch when she dropped off her kids for their weekend visit. In a calm way, Natalya instructed her nanny that she was not allowed to let her husband's ex-wife into their home, let alone offer her a meal. She told her husband that she would not tolerate these intrusions to her space any longer, and he readily agreed that his ex-wife's behavior was a boundary violation of which he did not approve. She then called her husband's ex-wife and calmly told her to please drop her children off by the front door from now on. She was able to communicate with everyone by doing the waltz of intimacy.

Limit Interactions

There are different ways to maintain clear boundaries. Some stepcouples, like Maya and Liam, Emma and Amir, and Natalya and her husband, establish rules to keep others at bay. Others choose to remove themselves from harmful situations.

Gay and lesbian couples face the same regenerated family challenges as heterosexual ones. Scarlett and Annabelle were both secure and able to dance the waltz of intimacy when dealing with a boundary violation committed by Annabelle's former girlfriend. When Scarlett first married Annabelle, she wanted to be kept in the loop with regard to information about her stepdaughter and schedule changes. She asked if she could read all the emails and texts between Annabelle and her former girlfriend. Annabelle was happy to share this information since she wanted to create a totally open and honest relationship with Scarlett. Very quickly, Scarlett grew disturbed that Annabelle's ex referred to Scarlett as "your future ex-wife" and signed every email with the moniker "your sexy ex." Scarlett wasn't jealous of this woman. She knew that Annabelle's former partner was doing this to annoy both of them rather than arouse romantic interest. However, she was disturbed that this woman could get away with inappropriate behavior without suffering any consequences. It just wasn't fair.

To protect herself from further aggravation, Scarlett chose to stop reading all texts and emails from Annabelle's ex-girlfriend. She asked Annabelle to tell her about schedule changes and news about her stepdaughter. She also asked her to tell her ex to stop goading them. In a calm, rational manner, she said, "Please tell your ex to stop signing emails and texts with 'your sexy ex.' It's inappropriate."

Annabelle totally agreed with Scarlett's assessment that her former partner was being inappropriate, but she disagreed with the strategy Scarlett suggested. She felt her ex would be delighted to know she was causing trouble and would act out even more. Annabelle said she would ignore any texts or messages that ended with the moniker "your sexy ex." She would only answer ones that did not include this sign-off. This was a passive way to communicate that she wouldn't respond to inappropriate messages. She also suggested that they use an online site, such as ourfamilywizard.com, to manage schedules, which would limit the number of texts and emails between households. Scarlett was satisfied with this solution.

While Scarlett chose to stop reading texts and emails from Annabelle's ex-girlfriend to preserve her boundaries, other secure partners may need to limit their exposure to other harmful violations. They may have to limit the number of their stepchildren's events or conferences they attend if they experience discomfort. Many stepparents want to support their stepchildren by attending all their soccer or volleyball games but are exposed to cold stares or petty comments by their partner's exes and the exes' friends. In situations where you cannot be protected from this, be discerning about which ones to attend. You don't have to be miserable while demonstrating your love to your stepchildren. Of course, you will attend celebrations such as graduations or weddings, but it isn't necessary to attend every extracurricular activity. You can tell your stepchildren that while you care about them very much and hope they do well, you will be rooting for them in spirit rather than in person. You don't have to share your reasons with them. They probably are old enough to feel their parent's negative feelings toward you and actually may be relieved by your absence.

Consistency Is Key

Before establishing a boundary, make sure you will be able to enforce it. Consistency is very important to maintaining healthy boundaries. For example, once you resolve that you will no longer reply to someone's emails, you must stick to this decision to maintain credibility. If you ignore four messages and then answer the fifth one out of frustration, unwittingly, you reinforce this person's behavior rather than curtail it. He will realize you ignore most emails but will respond occasionally. He will then hound you with more messages, expecting you to respond intermittently.

Not only do healthy boundaries protect us from harm, they also protect our relationships from the intrusions of others. They are necessary for our survival.

20

BALANCE POWER IN
YOUR RELATIONSHIP

For any relationship to thrive, it must be fair and equitable to both partners. Each partner should have equal access to resources, and household responsibilities should be fairly divided. This doesn't mean chores must be divided 50/50; instead, relationship equity means both partners feel that they are putting forth equal effort toward maintaining the welfare of their relationship. Furthermore, each partner trusts that the other respects his or her opinions and needs and considers these opinions and needs when making decisions. Research has found that couples who have an equitable relationship and share power are happy and satisfied with their relationships.[1]

Many stepcouples fall short of achieving relationship equity. When one or both partners adopt certain cultural norms—men are superior to women or a woman's role and place in the family is to please and defer to her partner, for instance—those norms powerfully influence the partners' attitudes and behaviors. Such antiquated beliefs skew the power in favor of the man, which is ultimately detrimental to the long-term stability of a heterosexual relationship. Dr. John Gottman found that heterosexual relationships are more likely to end when a man has more power than a woman and to last when a woman is as influential as her partner.[2]

Dr. Gottman and colleagues also found that homosexual couples may have something to teach heterosexual ones regarding relationship equity.[3] Their research showed that while both groups share similar problems, homosexual partners are more aware that love and power are interconnected and consequently tend to treat each other more respectfully during conflicts. They begin conversations less harshly and use humor and affection to deflect arising tensions more than heterosexual couples do. They also are more open to satisfying each other's needs and opinions, ensuring that both partners are treated fairly.

SOURCES OF POWER IMBALANCES

Power imbalances in stepcouple relationships can stem from specific regenerated family dynamics. The complaint I've heard most often is from a stepparent who is encouraged to assume many child-care responsibilities for her partner's children but isn't given any power to establish and maintain household rules or correct the stepchildren when they misbehave. The biological parent defends this decision by saying, "You aren't a parent. I know what's best for my children," or "You don't know what's best for my children. I do." As a result, many stepparents end up feeling overworked, exhausted, and powerless, leading to resentment and frustration. Accumulated resentment is a primary reason some partners end their relationships.

Another dynamic that creates a power imbalance is when a biological parent, despite being in a new relationship, insists on doing things the old way "for the sake of my children." He may be unwilling to move to a new home or adopt new holiday traditions, fearing that any change in structure or routine will traumatize the children. The new stepparent, who also does not want to hurt them, defers to her partner's wishes and ends up dreading holidays or vacations that she used to enjoy. Much to her chagrin, one stepmother went on her honeymoon with her nine-year-old stepdaughter because her husband had taken her on all previous vacations. It wasn't the way this stepmother wanted to begin her marriage, to say the least!

Another stepmother described her situation this way: "My husband came with lots of baggage, while I only had a carry-on." Some stepcouples lack equity because one partner's financial constraints, a difficult ex-partner, or a sick child demand an excessive amount of a stepcouple's time, attention, and other resources. Catering to this "baggage" can lead the less burdened partner to sacrifice so many of their beloved activities and friendships that they experience little joy in everyday life. When the benefits of a relationship no longer outweigh the costs, a partner is likely to end the relationship.

Strangely enough, both partners can feel powerless at the same time. How is this possible? Your perception of your empowerment affects your emotional state more than the actual power you have. Each partner can believe that the other one holds all the power in the relationship and end up feeling depressed or anxious.[4] If unaddressed, this imbalance of power, either real or imagined, can create serious problems for stepcouples.

Do you feel your relationship is fair? Ask yourself these questions:

- Do you and your partner consider each other's needs and opinions as much as your own? Are each of your dreams and goals an afterthought in the other's mind?
- Have you or your partner given up your identity in service of your relationship? Do you or your partner no longer engage in activities that defined who you were?
- Do you or your partner feel you are living more in the other's world rather than creating a shared one?
- Are you or your partner continually giving in to things you don't really want to do?
- Do you or your partner feel you never get your way? Does one of you occasionally throw tantrums or break down crying and screaming when things don't go your way?
- Do you or your partner feel it's acceptable to take your temper out on the other? Or does one of you feel forced to listen to the other's angry outbursts?

A note of caution: I will show you how to address relationship inequity by communicating with your partner securely. However, in cases where one partner exerts control in abusive ways—through intimidation, threats, coercion, mental cruelty, physical punishment, or isolation, for example—learning to communicate more effectively will not correct the power imbalance. The abused partner needs to seek professional help to prevent further victimization.

ADDRESSING RELATIONSHIP INEQUITY

Over time, some stepcouple relationships become more equitable as custody battles are resolved or finances improve, for example. Unfortunately, this isn't the case for all stepcouples; their problems can last for a long, long time. Then depression and anxiety can develop so gradually that a partner may not recognize it until it's serious. Here's an example of how this happened to two stepmothers, Brianna and Melissa, whose stepsons "failed to launch" from home. Both married their partners when their stepsons were about 10 years old. At a young age, both boys had been diagnosed with learning disabilities and had received specialized tutoring to help them with schoolwork. They were admitted to college, but one dropped out and the other one flunked out after his sophomore year. They both moved back home and stayed in their bedrooms playing video games for hours on end.

When their stepsons were adolescents, both Brianna and Melissa were active full-time stepmothers, helping the boys with difficult academic subjects along with taking care of their other needs. They had looked forward to having an empty nest and spending more alone time with their partners but gladly welcomed their stepsons home to regroup after their disappointing college experiences. However, they didn't imagine that their stepsons might live with them indefinitely. After several months, neither stepson seemed to care about what he might do in the future or made any attempt to get a part-time job. Nor did their fathers push them to clean up their messes or find a job. Because of the added responsibilities and the lack of control they experienced in their homes, Brianna and Melissa grew depressed and anxious and decided to broach their unhappiness with their partners.

While these two stepmothers shared a similar problem, they discussed it very differently with their husbands because each couple had different attachment styles. Brianna and her husband, Jonah, were anxious/avoidant, while Melissa and her partner, Ethan, were both secure.

Brianna was very angry that Jonah's avoidant tendencies prevented him from taking steps to help her stepson become a self-sufficient adult. After asking him multiple times to talk to his son about helping around the apartment, Brianna yelled at Jonah for never finding the time to sit down and have a serious conversation with his son. She did not understand how Jonah could idly stand by without telling his son to take his dirty plates to the sink. Why did he think it was acceptable for Brianna to pick up after his son? And why did he seem so unconcerned that his son lacked the necessary life skills to take care of himself?

Brianna felt controlled by Jonah's passivity and blamed his lax parenting style for her stepson's lack of motivation to take charge of his life.

She was so angry that by the time she talked to Jonah, she was belligerent, domineering, and whiny, hoping this would spur him to take action to help his son. Not surprisingly, he didn't respond well to what she said and shut down emotionally. Neither felt good after their conversation.

Jonah did not realize his passivity was controlling Brianna's life. His avoidant emotional style prevented him from thinking about the sacrifices Brianna was making on his son's behalf. He just took for granted what Brianna did for his son, never expressed any gratitude, and had little compassion for what she was going through. Secure partners, on the other hand, are better able to identify what their partners are experiencing; they also are more open to listening to and being influenced by their suggestions.

Since Melissa and Ethan were secure, their conversation was harmonious. She prefaced her comments with a statement of love. She told Ethan that she loved him and her stepson very much. Then she added that she was worried her stepson lacked direction and could end up spending the rest of his life in his room if he didn't receive help for his emotional problems and wasn't encouraged to find a job. Plus, she didn't think it was fair for Ethan to expect her to clean up his son's messes. She had reached her limit and wasn't willing to do it any longer. Ethan implemented several strategies to handle these relationship inequities, as we'll see below.

Acknowledge Imbalance

Ethan calmly listened to Melissa without reacting defensively. He said he knew his son had problems and had hoped time, by itself, would help him mature. He realized he hadn't been sufficiently proactive in getting his son the help he needed and promised to take his son for a psychiatric evaluation. He also told Melissa that he was very grateful for the help she had provided, but he would take over her chores or make sure his son did them.

Melissa felt much better after Ethan acknowledged her feelings, addressed the imbalance in their relationship, and tried to correct it to the best of his abilities. By promising to get help for his son, he gave Melissa hope that positive changes were going to take place.

"You've Got Points"

Secure partners handle conflict with grace and humor. During their conversation, Ethan told Melissa she had millions of points accruing in her bank account as a result of dealing with his son. This was his lighthearted way to validate her experience as well as to defuse the tension she was feeling. Humor can lower stress levels.

Give Up Control

Ethan also told Melissa he understood that she was frustrated by the fact that his son did not suffer any consequences for failing to put his dishes in the sink or clean up after himself. He accepted responsibility for enabling this situation to continue for far too long. He asked Melissa if she had any suggestions for getting his son to do his fair share of household chores. She thought money might motivate him. Ethan gave his son an allowance of $60 a week. From this money, Melissa recommended they deduct $1 each time they completed a chore on his son's behalf.

At dinner that night, Ethan told his son why they were imposing a fine if he didn't clean up his messes. After all, he was a member of the household who had to pitch in; Melissa and he were not his staff whose job was to serve him. From now on, they would be paid to do any chore that was rightfully his. Ethan's son accepted this new policy without complaint. As Melissa predicted, he did not want to give up any of his weekly allowance and began to clean up his messes. This change delighted her and helped her reestablish control of her living space.

Teamwork

When stepcouples experience chronic problems, good communication is essential. By itself, communication may not be sufficient to solve stepcouples' problems, but it can prevent them (and any resulting inequity) from escalating and causing further damage to their emotional bond. Treating each other with kindness and compassion during a conflict—dancing the waltz of intimacy—allows stepcouples to discuss their problems in an open and cooperative manner and ensures they will continue to feel safe and secure with each other.

A CASE ILLUSTRATION

The following example demonstrates the therapeutic process by which one stepcouple worked through an equity imbalance in their relationship.

Jordana needed to live in the city that was close to the facility where her son, who had a certain medical condition, resided. Her second husband, Drew, understood her decision and moved into her apartment when they married. However, he loved spending time outdoors hiking and rock climbing and felt trapped in an urban environment. After a few years, he increasingly felt physically and emotionally unhealthy and began to think leaving Jordana was the only way to regain some happiness. To prevent this, he asked her to accompany him to couples therapy.

Identify the Conflict

During the first session, I asked them what brought them to my office and what they hoped to accomplish. Drew said he felt trapped between a rock and a hard place: his love for Jordana and his need to spend time in nature. He didn't feel as though he could postpone gratifying his desire to be outdoors any longer, yet he loved Jordana very much and would be miserable without her in his life. He didn't know what to do.

Jordana said she felt terrible that Drew was unhappy and wished she could accommodate his dream of living in the country, but could not. He knew from the moment they got involved with each other that she would never move. She didn't think it fair of him to keep asking and was annoyed by his persistence.

Drew and Jordana both said they resented each other, and they had grown emotionally distant because of their fights about where to live. They described a pattern to these fights (that we can recognize as the stepcouple shuffle): Drew would complain about something that bothered him about city life, Jordana would briefly listen, then grow defensive and cut him off. Their conversations ended with both feeling isolated and misunderstood. They hoped counseling would help them let go of these resentments, emotionally reconnect, and resolve their impasse.

Identify Unacknowledged Emotions

For partners to meet each other's needs, they must first understand what the needs are. Drew shared that his brother had been his parents' favored child, and he believed Jordana loved her son more than she loved him. He realized he unconsciously instigated many of their fights to test whom she loved more. These fights confirmed his belief that he was second best; the more times Drew complained about the city's traffic, noise, and dirt, the less Jordana sympathized with his unhappiness.

Jordana was surprised to learn that Drew wasn't just complaining about living in the city; he also was indirectly expressing a feeling of insecurity about whether she truly loved him. This insight made her realize she hadn't been fulfilling his need to feel loved, and she promised him she would be more loving and affectionate in the future.

During these sessions, Jordana also revealed some of her deepest fears. She shared that the more Drew complained about the city, the more her insecurities grew. Before meeting him, she worried that no man would take on her "baggage." Her ex-husband had divorced her because he couldn't accept his son's disabilities. She had felt lucky that Drew accepted her son. Now she wondered whether he was turning out to be as self-centered as her ex-husband and feared that it was only a matter of time before he too abandoned her.

Promote Understanding and Acceptance

Counseling helps partners see their problems from a different perspective. Drew and Jordana were not just fighting about where to live. Without realizing it, they had been struggling to feel safe and secure with each other.

Drew was as unaware as Jordana that he had triggered her fear of abandonment. While his complaints were a way of sharing his feelings about the city with Jordana, he now realized they had increased her insecurities and created an emotional wedge between them. In counseling, he had two revelations: (1) if he was going to complain about something that Jordana could not change, he also had to reassure her that he loved her very much, and (2) the more he complained, the unhappier he was. He had to stop complaining and make the best of his situation. His love for Jordana trumped his love of nature.

As Drew and Jordana recognized each other's underlying fears, they felt greater compassion for each other, which defused much of their anger and resentment. Plus, they learned to help each other feel more secure by frequently expressing their love for each other.

Rebuild Trust

Over the course of therapy, Drew and Jordana grew to trust each other, which allowed them to drop their defenses and become more vulnerable and open. With less need to defend themselves, they were able to listen to each other speak without interrupting. When one would try to interject an opinion while the other was talking, I would remind them that each would get their turn to speak; it wasn't necessary to explain or defend oneself at that moment.

I also requested that before they took their turn stating their positions, they acknowledge what the other had said. As I mentioned previously, this is an important step in the communication process that is often skipped. Partners need to know their messages have been accurately heard and understood. While Jordana couldn't give Drew a country life, she could tell him she understood how much nature meant to him and was genuinely sorry he wasn't getting enough of it. She was able to thank him for the sacrifice he was making for her and promise him that she would be willing to spend at least two weekends a month in the country with him.

Choose Reality over Fantasy

Drew felt much better knowing Jordana understood his needs, even if she couldn't fulfill all of them. He realized that he had been negotiating for an impossible goal, which only frustrated and disappointed him and placed a wedge between him and Jordana. It was time to stop working toward something unachievable and focus his efforts on a pathway to success.

Behave as Teammates

Drew and Jordana had fundamentally different needs that could not be equally satisfied. Jordana's need to be close to her son overruled Drew's love of nature. Yet these differences did not have to drive them apart. By becoming sensitive to each other's need to feel safe and secure, they were able to communicate very differently about their differences. With kindness, love, and respect as a solid foundation, they could behave as teammates rather than adversaries, resulting in greater ease in discussing and resolving issues.

21

FURTHER STEPS

As illustrated in the last few chapters, stepcouples face many challenges. However, insider/outsider issues, boundary violations, and power imbalances are not the true culprits that tear stepcouple relationships apart. I believe that unrealistic expectations and a clash of attachment styles during conflicts bear the brunt of the blame for eroding partners' trust in each other and for weakening their emotional connection. This book gives you the tools for a vibrant, loving relationship by helping you determine whether your stepfamily expectations are realistic and by teaching you how to communicate during conflicts in ways that protect each other's feelings of safety and security. This will enable you to navigate complex stepfamily dynamics with confidence and kindness, allowing you and your partner to build a happy, fulfilling life together. Please keep this book handy for future reference.

To maintain your progress in getting your relationship back on solid footing, consider doing one or more of the following activities.

STEPCOUPLES COUNSELING

Going to stepcouples counseling with a licensed marriage and family therapist may help you and your partner. In a safe and neutral setting, a couples therapist can help you gain more awareness into your relationship, modify any dysfunctional interactions, and resolve existing conflicts. Couples counseling can also help accentuate the strengths in your relationship and enhance your intimacy.

For couples counseling to be successful, both partners must be committed to the process. And since you must form an alliance with your therapist toward achieving this goal, it's important to select one with whom you share a good rapport and who has the necessary skills to help you.

When choosing a couples therapist, there are several factors to consider. All psychotherapists need to be good listeners and to be empathic. In addition, marriage and family therapists need specialized training to understand the unique dynamics of couples in order to help them overcome their differences. If possible, you want to select a therapist who specifically trained as a couples therapist. The American Association for Marriage and Family Therapy is a great resource for finding a therapist. Its website (www.aamft.org) contains a state-by-state referral panel of licensed marriage and family therapists.

In your initial phone call, find out whether the therapist is licensed, takes your insurance, and has time to meet with you, and ask about his or her particular qualifications and approach to couples counseling. Ideally you want to work with a therapist who has been trained in a form of couples counseling that strives to deepen the emotional connection between you and your partner. I recommend the following approaches:

- **Emotionally Focused Therapy:** Developed by Canadian psychologist Dr. Sue Johnson, emotionally focused therapy (EFT) is based on the belief that human beings need strong emotional bonds with others to thrive. Partners experience relationship distress and grow more insecure and distant from each other when their bond is damaged by conflicts that trigger their childhood fears of abandonment. The goal of EFT is to repair a couple's emotional connection by helping them understand and reorganize each of their emotional responses to conflicts and become sensitive to the other's responses as well.
- **The Gottman Method:** The goal of Gottman Method Couples Therapy is to increase affection, closeness, and respect between partners by teaching them the skills needed to sustain a strong relationship. After nearly 40 years of research, Dr. John Gottman and his colleagues have identified the positive elements that enhance a relationship as well as the negative ones that harm a couple's emotional connection. In sessions, couples are instructed

on how to behave in ways that lead to greater intimacy and satisfaction along with how to limit damaging behaviors, such as
contempt. When positive interactions outweigh negative ones,
partners can manage conflict, provide each other with love and
respect, turn toward each other to get their needs met, and support each other's dreams.

- **Positive Psychology:** Founded in 1998 by psychologist Martin
  E. P. Seligman of the University of Pennsylvania, this form of
  therapy accentuates the importance of increasing positive emotions, human strengths, and meaningful interactions between
  partners. Research has found that thriving couples focus on
  the positive aspects of life more than couples who split up or
  unhappily stay together do. Not only do they cope well during
  hardship, they also build more bright points into their lives. In
  positive couples psychotherapy, partners learn to highlight positive emotions and live in the present moment.
- **Imago Relationship Therapy:** Taken from the Latin word
  for "image," imago relationship therapy was codeveloped by Dr.
  Harville Hendrix and Dr. Helen LaKelly Hunt. They hypoth-
  esize that based on childhood experiences, adults hold on to an
  unconscious construct (or image) of love from which they develop specific behaviors to maintain love and stay safe. Relationship dissatisfaction and frustration often occurs when one partner
  does not conform to the other's images of what love should be.
  In imago relationship therapy, couples examine the root cause
  of their unhappiness. They are then equipped with tools to heal
  childhood wounds and relate to each other in healthier ways.

Regardless of the specific therapeutic approach, in my opinion, it's
very important to work with a therapist who understands and embraces
the unique qualities of stepfamilies in order to understand the context
in which you are struggling. Feel free to ask a therapist these questions:

- How much experience do you have working with stepcouples?
- How does your approach differ from working with couples from
  intact families?

• Are you a stepfamily member? Without being too personal, has your experience been positive or negative?

After an initial visit, if you have any hesitations about continuing to work with the therapist you've seen, try another one. You may need to go to a few before finding one with whom you feel comfortable and one you believe can help you overcome your relationship problems.

COUPLES SEMINARS AND RETREATS

Attending a course, seminar, or weekend relationship retreat is another way to deepen your compassion for each other. Many community centers, religious institutions, and psychology programs, such as the Gottman Institute, offer lectures, classes, or weekend retreats for couples. Many psychologists also offer online webinars that are very instructive.

SUPPORT GROUPS

If you haven't participated in a peer support group, you may be surprised to find how helpful they are in providing support, acknowledgment, and advice from those who understand what you are going through. Despite the prevalence of stepfamilies in society, many stepcouples complain that they don't know any other couples with stepchildren. Afraid to share their experience with family and friends who may be unable to relate to, or may be critical of, what they are going through, they end up feeling isolated and stigmatized. If you feel this way, joining a support group can help you feel less alone and more understood by others, making it easier to deal with family challenges.

In support groups no one member holds greater power or authority. When you share your problems with others in this democratic environment, your anxiety can be reduced and your self-esteem and overall sense of well-being can improve. Additionally, other members can serve as role models to inspire and encourage you.

There are two main types of support groups: online and in-person.

Online Support Groups

You may want to join an online group. Search for one by "step-couple," "remarried couple," or "repartnered with children."

Like anything else, online support groups have benefits and risks. Similar to an in-person support group, members in online groups share information and support and encourage each other. One unique benefit of an online group is that you don't have to leave the comfort of your home and can participate at any time of day or night. Another advantage is that you don't have to disclose your identity. While it's important to always remember that online support groups are public and that anyone in the world can read the messages you post, you can pick a nickname with which to be identified.

There are a few drawbacks to online groups to be aware of. Before taking advice from a support group member, exercise caution. Since you have limited information about the members' past experiences, make sure you know that their advice is applicable to your situation before following it. Steer clear of online communities that are overly negative, and join one whose members are positive and respectful.

It's not always easy to express oneself clearly and concisely in written form. Therefore, some online messages unintentionally may be misleading and confusing. Double-check that you are accurately interpreting each one. And one final note of caution: be careful that no one takes advantage of you. While this may be rare, online communities are susceptible to predatory, unscrupulous individuals whose intent is to promote a product or commit fraud.

In-Person Support Groups

You may prefer to join an in-person support group. You may be able to find information about an ongoing one from therapists or mental health clinics in your neighborhood. Also, look for notices about upcoming meetings in local papers and on bulletin boards in community centers and places of worship. You can conduct an online search for one by pairing where you reside with the term "stepcouple support group."

If you can't find a stepcouple support group in your neighborhood, you may want to form your own. How do you go about this?

DECIDE ON THE DETAILS

Here are some questions to consider before setting up a support group:

- Where will meetings be held? Most support groups are held in churches, libraries, community centers, or hospitals that provide free rooms or charge a nominal fee. Select a room that holds slightly more people than the number of members you expect to attend. Too big of a meeting space can feel cavernous and empty, while one that is too small can feel cramped and uncomfortable. To encourage everyone to participate, arrange chairs in a circle.
- How many members will participate in the support group? It's best to have a group that's large enough to function if some of the members are absent but small enough for members to feel comfortable to share. Strive to get five to 15 members to join your group; anything larger can become unmanageable and impersonal.
- Who is eligible to attend the support group? Is it necessary for both partners in a stepcouple relationship to attend a meeting, or can one partner attend alone? Do you want only members who are in a stepcouple relationship, or is it acceptable to include someone who is thinking about getting involved with a partner who has children from a prior relationship? Will attendance be mandatory or voluntary?
- At what time and how often will the group meet? Will the group meet during the day or evening, and during the week or weekend? Will the meeting be held once a week, once every two weeks, or once a month?
- How long will meetings last? Most meetings run for an hour and a half to two hours.
- What format will the meeting have? Will meetings consist of free-flowing discussions, or will a specific topic be chosen to discuss at each one?
- Will a facilitator or moderator lead the meeting?
- Will meetings be free? If not, how much will each one cost?

ESTABLISH GROUND RULES

For a support group to succeed, members must follow certain guidelines during each meeting. Consider implementing the following:

- First and foremost, confidentiality must be maintained. What members say in the room must stay in the room. For members to share intimate details of their lives, they must trust that everyone in the group will be discreet and never reveal anything that is said during a meeting to anyone who does not belong to it.
- Group members will abide by good communication skills during meetings. Members will be instructed to listen to each other without interruption and to respond to each other with empathy and acceptance. They will avoid making judgmental and critical comments. While everyone in the group will be encouraged to participate, if anyone chooses to remain silent, the other group members will respect this decision.
- Group members will appreciate that all members are entitled to their feelings and perspectives and are responsible for deciding how to best handle their situation.
- Members will respect each other's boundaries.
- Members will avoid using offensive language.

RECRUIT MEMBERS

To find other members to join your support group, ask local clergy, doctors, and mental health clinics to refer people who they believe would benefit from it. Advertise the group in a community online forum and in the local paper.

I hope all these suggestions will help you and your partner continue to strengthen your relationship.

CLOSING WORDS

Thank you for reading *The Happy Stepcouple*. I am pleased to have shared with you my ideas about how to improve your relationship. I hope you tried many of the exercises throughout *The Happy Stepcouple*, which form the foundation of communicating more kindly and compassionately with your partner. With these insights and skills, you will feel more secure in your relationship and be better able to navigate any family problems you experience.

It is my hope that this book has given you the courage, hope, and tools you need to overcome the challenges of stepcouplehood. I wish you the best of luck on your journey to find contentment and peace with your partner.

ACKNOWLEDGMENTS

Writing a book is a labor of love that requires commitment, patience, and perseverance. I am grateful to so many people whose support and encouragement enabled me to complete this project.

First, I would like to thank the many stepcouples with whom I worked in my private practice. They inspired me to write this book; they taught me so much, and they added meaning to my life. I am privileged that they trusted me by sharing intimate details of their lives. The bonds we forged during these journeys are very special to me. While I wish I could thank each couple by name, to preserve their confidentiality, they shall remain anonymous. I hope they know who they are and how grateful I am to them.

Also, I would like to thank the more than 1,200 people who completed my lengthy online questionnaire titled The Successful Stepfamilies Research Project. By sharing their personal experiences, they helped me understand the diverse struggles so many stepcouples face and helped me organize the contents of this book in what I hope is a clear way.

I would like to acknowledge the academic foundation upon which this book is based. My work as a psychotherapist has been influenced by the ideas and research of many brilliant and skilled theoreticians and clinicians. I am most indebted to two giants in the field: Dr. John Gottman, whose 40 years of marital research has led to a deep understanding of the relationship dynamics that strengthen or weaken emotional ties between partners; and Dr. Sue Johnson, who developed emotionally focused therapy, a form of couples therapy that focuses on helping couples repair their emotional connection with each other. I have incorporated many of their ideas and techniques in my work as a couples therapist and am very grateful to Dr. Gottman and Dr. Johnson for their guidance and wisdom.

Many hands and eyes pass over a book before its completion. I want to thank Joelle Delbourgo, my literary agent, for championing this book from the very beginning. She recommended I use Molly Lyons to edit this book, and I could not have chosen a more skillful and lovely editor. Molly is so intelligent, competent, and responsible. It truly has been a joyous experience working with her. I also want to thank Rona Bernstein, Psy.D., for copy editing my book. She, too, is smart, caring, and capable; I am so fortunate to have had her assistance. Both Molly and Rona immeasurably improved my book, and I could not have completed this project without their help. I am also grateful to Suzanne Staszak-Silva and the staff at Rowman & Littlefield for placing their faith in me.

During the entire process of writing this book, I received lots of love, kindness, and support from many family and friends. In particular, I want to thank my loving and generous parents, Estelle and Leo, as well as my husband, Ronnie. He read each iteration of every chapter and offered excellent suggestions to improve them. He truly is a good sport, allowing me to write about experiences from our marriage to benefit the readers of this book. I dedicate this book to him.

From the bottom of my heart, thank you all!

R. K.

Appendix A

PETERSON AND SELIGMAN'S LIST OF VIRTUES AND CHARACTER STRENGTHS

This is the complete list of Peterson and Seligman's character strengths described in chapter 10.[1]

CLASSIFICATION OF CHARACTER STRENGTHS

1. ***Wisdom and knowledge***—cognitive strengths that entail the acquisition and use of knowledge

   Creativity [originality, ingenuity]: Thinking of novel and productive ways to conceptualize and do things; includes artistic achievement but is not limited to it

   Curiosity [interest, novelty-seeking, openness to experience]: Taking an interest in ongoing experience for its own sake; finding subjects and topics fascinating; exploring and discovering

   Open-mindedness [judgment, critical thinking]: Thinking things through and examining them from all sides; not jumping to conclusions; being able to change one's mind in light of evidence; weighing all evidence fairly

   Love of learning: Mastering new skills, topics, and bodies of knowledge, whether on one's own or formally; obviously related to the strength of curiosity but goes beyond it to describe the tendency to add systematically to what one knows

   Perspective [wisdom]: Being able to provide wise counsel to others; having ways of looking at the world that make sense to oneself and to other people

2. *Courage*—emotional strengths that involve the exercise of will to accomplish goals in the face of opposition, external or internal

Bravery [valor]: Not shrinking from threat, challenge, difficulty, or pain; speaking up for what is right even if there is opposition; acting on convictions even if unpopular; includes physical bravery but is not limited to it

Persistence [perseverance, industriousness]: Finishing what one starts; persisting in a course of action in spite of obstacles; "getting it out the door"; taking pleasure in completing tasks

Integrity [authenticity, honesty]: Speaking the truth but more broadly presenting oneself in a genuine way and acting in a sincere way; being without pretense; taking responsibility for one's feelings and actions

Vitality [zest, enthusiasm, vigor, energy]: Approaching life with excitement and energy; not doing things halfway or halfheartedly; living life as an adventure; feeling alive and activated

3. *Humanity*—interpersonal strengths that involve tending and befriending others

Love: Valuing close relations with others, in particular those in which sharing and caring are reciprocated; being close to people

Kindness [generosity, nurturance, care, compassion, altruistic love, "niceness"]: Doing favors and good deeds for others; helping them; taking care of them

Social intelligence [emotional intelligence, personal intelligence]: Being aware of the motives and feelings of other people and oneself; knowing what to do to fit into different social situations; knowing what makes other people tick

4. *Justice*—civic strengths that underlie healthy community life

Citizenship [social responsibility, loyalty, teamwork]: Working well as a member of a group or team; being loyal to the group; doing one's share

Fairness: Treating all people the same according to notions of fairness and justice; not letting personal feelings bias decisions about others; giving everyone a fair chance

Leadership: Encouraging a group of which one is a member to get things done and at the same maintain time good relations within the group; organizing group activities and seeing that they happen

5. *Temperance*—strengths that protect against excess

Forgiveness and mercy: Forgiving those who have done wrong; accepting the shortcomings of others; giving people a second chance; not being vengeful

Humility/modesty: Letting one's accomplishments speak for themselves; not seeking the spotlight; not regarding oneself as more special than one is

Prudence: Being careful about one's choices; not taking undue risks; not saying or doing things that might later be regretted

Self-regulation [self-control]: Regulating what one feels and does; being disciplined; controlling one's appetites and emotions

6. *Transcendence*—strengths that forge connections to the larger universe and provide meaning

Appreciation of beauty and excellence [awe, wonder, elevation]: Noticing and appreciating beauty, excellence, and/or skilled performance in various domains of life, from nature to art to mathematics to science to everyday experience

Gratitude: Being aware of and thankful for the good things that happen; taking time to express thanks

Hope [optimism, future-mindedness, future orientation]: Expecting the best in the future and working to achieve it; believing that a good future is something that can be brought about

Humor [playfulness]: Liking to laugh and tease; bringing smiles to other people; seeing the light side; making (not necessarily telling) jokes

Spirituality [religiousness, faith, purpose]: Having coherent beliefs about the higher purpose and meaning of the universe; knowing where one fits within the larger scheme; having beliefs about the meaning of life that shape conduct and provide comfort

NOTES

INTRODUCTION

1. Mavis Hetherington and John Kelly, *For Better or Worse: Divorce Reconsidered* (New York: W.W. Norton, 2002), 165.

2. Pew Research Center, *Parenting in America: Outlook, Worries, Aspirations Are Strongly Linked to Financial Situation*, December 17, 2015.

CHAPTER 1: STEPFAMILY FALLACIES

1. Lawrence Ganong and Marilyn Coleman, *Stepfamily Relationships: Development, Dynamics, and Intervention* (New York: Springer, 2004), 161.

2. Mavis Hetherington and John Kelly, *For Better or Worse: Divorce Reconsidered* (New York: W.W. Norton, 2002), 232.

3. Constance Ahrons, *The Good Divorce* (New York: HarperCollins, 1994), 233.

4. Ibid., 73.

CHAPTER 2: EXPECTATIONS OF YOUR RELATIONSHIP

1. Gary Chapman, *Five Languages of Love* (Chicago: Northfield Publishing, 2015).

2. Terri Orbuch, *Finding Love Again: 6 Simple Steps to a New and Happy Relationship* (Naperville, IL: Sourcebooks Casablanca, 2012).

3. Shelly L. Gable et al., "Safely Testing the Alarm: Close Other's Responses to Personal Positive Events," *Journal of Personality and Social Psychology* 103, no. 6 (2012): 965.

4. Christian Elabd et al., "Oxytocin Is an Age-Specific Circulating Hormone That Is Necessary for Muscle Maintenance and Regeneration," *Nature Communications* 5 (June 2014): 4082.

5. Anik Debrot et al., "Touch as an Interpersonal Emotion Regulation Process in Couples' Daily Lives: The Mediating Role of Psychological Intimacy," *Personality and Social Psychology Bulletin* 39, no. 10 (July 2013): 1376.

6. Arthur Aron et al., "Couples' Shared Participation in Novel and Arousing Activities and Experienced Relationship Quality," *Journal of Personality and Social Psychology* 78 (March 2000): 281.

CHAPTER 4: REDEFINE THE ROLE OF STEPPARENT

1. E. Mavis Hetherington and John Kelly, *For Better or Worse: Divorce Reconsidered* (New York: W.W. Norton, 2002), 232.

CHAPTER 5: THE RELEVANCE OF EMOTIONAL ATTACHMENT STYLES FOR STEPCOUPLES

1. John Bowlby, *Attachment and Loss, Vol. 1: Attachment* (New York: Basic Books, 1969, 1982).

2. Mary D. Salter Ainsworth and Silvia M. Bell, "Attachment, Exploration, and Separation: Illustrated by the Behavior of One-Year-Olds in a Strange Situation," *Child Development* 41 (1970): 49–67.

3. Ibid.

4. Mary Main and Erik Hesse, "Parents' Unresolved Traumatic Experiences Are Related to Infant Disorganized Attachment Status: Is Frightened and/or Frightening Parental Behavior the Linking Mechanism?" In *Attachment in the Preschool Years: Theory Research and Intervention*, edited by M. Greenberg, D. Cicchetti, and E. M. Cummings (Chicago: University of Chicago Press, 1990), 163.

5. Cindy Hazan and Phillip R. Shaver, "Romantic Love Conceptualized as an Attachment Process," *Journal of Personality and Social Psychology* 52 (March 1987): 512.

6. Ibid., 515.

7. Cindy Hazan and Phillip R. Shaver, "Love and Work: An Attachment-Theoretical Perspective," *Journal of Personality and Social Psychology* 59 (August 1990): 278.

8. Mario Mikulincer and Phillip R. Shaver, *Attachment in Adulthood: Structure, Dynamics, and Change* (New York: Guilford Press, 2007), 29.

9. Phillip R. Shaver and Mario Mikulincer, "Attachment Theory and Research: Resurrection of the Psychodynamic Approach to Personality," *Journal of Research in Personality* 39 (February 2005): 26.

CHAPTER 6: UNDERSTAND EACH ATTACHMENT STYLE AND ITS UNIQUE COPING REACTION

1. Phillip R. Shaver and Mario Mikulincer, "Attachment Theory and Research: Resurrection of the Psychodynamic Approach to Personality," *Journal of Research in Personality* 39 (February 2005): 41.

2. Ibid.

CHAPTER 7: THE CLASH OF EMOTIONAL ATTACHMENT STYLES

1. James A. Coan, Hillary S. Schaefer, and Richard J. Davidson, "Lending a Hand: Social Regulation of the Neural Response to Threat," *Psychological Science* 2, no. 12 (December 2006): 1032–39.

2. Brooke C. Feeney and Roxanne L. Thrush, "Relationship Influences on Exploration in Adulthood: The Characteristics and Function of a Secure Base," *Journal of Personality and Social Psychology* 98 (January 2010): 71–74.

3. Heidemarie K. Laurent and Sally Powers, "Emotion Regulation in Emerging Adult Couples: Temperament, Attachment, and HPA Response to Conflict," *Biological Psychology* 76, nos. 1–2 (September 2007): 66–70.

4. Heidemarie K. Laurent and Sally I. Powers, "Social-Cognitive Predictors of Hypothalamic-Pituitary-Adrenal Reactivity to Interpersonal Conflict in Emerging Adult Couples," *Journal of Social and Personal Relationships* 23, no. 5 (October 2006): 703–20.

CHAPTER 9: BOLSTER YOUR SECURITY LEVEL

1. John Gottman and Nan Silver, *Why Marriages Succeed or Fail and How You Can Make Yours Last* (New York: Simon and Schuster, 1995), 79–81.

2. Barbara L. Fredrickson et al., "Open Hearts Build Lives: Positive Emotions, Induced through Loving-Kindness Meditation, Build Consequential

Personal Resources," *Journal of Personality and Social Psychology* 95, no. 5 (November 2008): 1058.

3. Shain-Ling Keng, Moira J. Smoski, and Clive J. Robins, "Effects of Mindfulness on Psychological Health: A Review of Empirical Studies," *Clinical Psychology Review* 31, no. 6 (August 2011): 1045.

4. Jon Kabat-Zinn, *Wherever You Go, There You Are* (New York: Hachette Books, 2005), 30.

5. Kevin Yackle et al., "Breathing Control Center Neurons That Promote Arousal in Mice," *Science* 31, no. 6332 (March 2017): 1414.

CHAPTER 10: MODIFY YOUR REACTIONS

1. Christopher Peterson and Martin E. P. Seligman, *Character Strengths and Virtues: A Handbook and Classification* (Oxford, UK: Oxford University Press, 2004).

2. Alex M. Wood et al., "Using Personal and Psychological Strengths Leads to Increases in Well-Being over Time: A Longitudinal Study and the Development of the Strengths Use Questionnaire," *Personality and Individual Differences* 50 (January 2011): 17.

CHAPTER 11: DON'T LET A GRUDGE WEIGH YOU DOWN

1. Stephanie Cacioppo, John P. Capitanio, and John T. Cacioppo, "Toward a Neurology of Loneliness," *Psychological Bulletin* 140, no. 6 (November 2014): 1465.

2. Julianne Holt-Lunstad et al., "Loneliness and Social Isolation as Risk Factors for Mortality: A Meta-analytic Review," *Perspectives on Psychological Science* 10, no. 2 (March 2015): 235.

3. Michelle Zheng et al., "The Unburdening Effects of Forgiveness: Effects on Slant Perception and Jumping Height," *Social Psychological and Personality Science* 6 (December 2015): 432–37.

4. Ian Williamson et al., "Forgiveness Aversion: Developing a Motivational State Measure of Perceived Forgiveness Risks," *Motivation and Emotion* 38, no. 3 (June 2014): 383.

5. Robert A. Emmons and Kevin E. McCullough, "Counting Blessings versus Burdens: An Experimental Investigation of Gratitude and Subjective Well-Being in Daily Life," *Journal of Personality and Social Psychology* 84, no. 2 (February 2003): 386.

6. Alex M. Wood et al., "Gratitude Influences Sleep through the Mechanism of Pre-sleep Cognitions," *Journal of Psychosomatic Research* 66 (January 2009): 46.

7. Monica Y. Bartlett and David DeSteno, "Gratitude and Prosocial Behavior: Helping When It Costs You," *Psychological Science* 17, no. 4 (April 2006): 324.

8. Jess Alberts and Angela Trethewey, "Love, Honor, and Thank," *Greater Good Magazine*, 2007, https://greatergood.berkeley.edu/article/item/love_honor_thank.

CHAPTER 12: GAIN COURAGE TO EXPRESS FEELINGS WITH CONFIDENCE

1. Dana R. Carney, Amy J. C. Cuddy, and Andy Yap, "Power Posing: Brief Nonverbal Displays Affect Neuroendocrine Levels and Risk Tolerance," *Psychological Science* 21 (September 2010): 1363–68.

2. Eva Ranehill et al., "Assessing the Robustness of Power Posing: No Effect on Hormones and Risk Tolerance in a Large Sample of Men and Women," *Psychological Science* 26, no. 5 (May 2015): 653–56.

CHAPTER 13: COMMUNICATE EFFECTIVELY

1. Robert Epstein et al., "Which Relationship Skills Count Most?" *Journal of Couple and Relationship Therapy* 12 (October 2013): 307.

2. Karina Schumann, "An Affirmed Self and a Better Apology: The Effect of Self-Affirmation on Transgressors' Responses to Victims," *Journal of Experimental Social Psychology* 54 (September 2014): 89–96.

3. Ibid.

4. Karina Schumann, "Does Love Mean Never Having to Say You're Sorry? Associations between Relationship Satisfaction, Perceived Apology Sincerity, and Forgiveness," *Journal of Social and Personal Relationships* 29 (June 2012): 1000.

CHAPTER 14: BOOST YOUR PARTNER'S SECURITY

1. Jeffrey Simpson and W. Steven Rholes, "Adult Attachment, Stress, and Romantic Relationships," *Current Opinion in Psychology* 13 (February 2017): 20.

2. Jeffrey A. Simpson and Nickola C. Overall, "Partner Buffering of Attachment Insecurity," *Current Directions in Psychological Science* 23 (February 2014): 56.

3. Benjamin Seider et al., "We Can Work It Out: Age Differences in Relational Pronouns, Physiology, and Behavior in Marital Conflict," *Psychology and Aging* 24, no. 3 (September 2009): 606.

4. John Gottman, Julie S. Gottman, and Joan DeClaire, *10 Lessons to Transform Your Marriage: America's Love Lab Experts Share Their Strategies for Strengthening Your Relationship* (New York: Crown, 2006), 236–39.

5. Emily Esfahani Smith, "The Masters of Love," *The Atlantic*, June 12, 2014.

CHAPTER 15: GO GENTLY INTO CONFLICT

1. Jeffrey A. Simpson, Steven Rholes, and Julia S. Nelligan, "Support Seeking and Support Giving within Couples in an Anxiety-Provoking Situation: The Role of Attachment Styles," *Journal of Personality and Social Psychology* 62 (January 1992): 434.

2. Nickola C. Overall, Jeffrey A. Simpson, and Helena Struthers, "Buffering Attachment-Related Avoidance: Softening Emotional and Behavioral Defenses during Conflict Discussions," *Journal of Personality and Social Psychology* 104, no. 5 (August 2013): 856.

3. Andreas Kappes and Tali Sharot, "The Automatic Nature of Motivated Belief Updating," *Behavioral Public Policy* (March 2018): 13.

4. Jeffrey A. Simpson, "Working Models of Attachment and Reactions to Different Forms of Caregiving from Romantic Partners," *Journal of Personality and Social Psychology* 93 (September 2007): 466–77.

5. John Gottman, Julie S. Gottman, and Joan DeClaire, *10 Lessons to Transform Your Marriage: America's Love Lab Experts Share Their Strategies for Strengthening Your Relationship* (New York: Crown, 2006), 180.

6. Allison K. Farrell et al., "Buffering the Responses of Avoidantly Attached Romantic Partners in Strain Test Situations," *Journal of Family Psychology* 30 (February 2016): 580.

7. Jessica E. Salvatore et al., "Recovering from Conflict in Romantic Relationships: A Developmental Perspective," *Psychological Science* 22 (March 2011): 381.

CHAPTER 16: DANCE THE WALTZ OF INTIMACY

1. Stephanie Wiebe et al., "Two-Year Follow-Up Outcomes in Emotionally Focused Couple Therapy: An Investigation of Relationship Satisfaction and Attachment Trajectories," *Journal of Marital and Family Therapy* 43, no. 2 (December 2016): 238.

2. Sue Johnson, *Hold Me Tight: Seven Conversations for a Lifetime of Love* (New York: Little, Brown and Company, 2008), 6–7.

3. Wiebe et al., 230.

4. James A. Coan, Hillary S. Schaefer, and Richard J. Davidson, "Lending a Hand: Social Regulation of the Neural Response to Threat," *Psychological Science* 2, no. 12 (December 2006): 1037.

5. Susan M. Johnson et al., "Soothing the Threatened Brain: Leveraging Contact Comfort with Emotionally Focused Therapy," *PLoS ONE* 8, no. 11 (2013): e79314, doi:10.1371/journal.pone.0079314.

CHAPTER 17: MANAGE INSIDER/OUTSIDER ISSUES

1. Kipling D. Williams, "The Pain of Exclusion," *Scientific American Mind* 21 (January/February 2011): 30–37.

2. Kipling D. Williams, "Ostracism," *Annual Review of Psychology* 58 (2007): 430.

3. Ibid., 433.

4. Roy F. Baumeister and Mark R. Leary, "The Need to Belong: Desire for Interpersonal Attachments as a Fundamental Human Motivation," *Psychological Bulletin* 117, no. 3 (May 1995): 511.

5. Williams, 2007, 445.

6. Lisa Zadro, Catherine Boland, and Rick Richardson, "How Long Does It Last? The Persistence of the Effects of Ostracism in the Socially Anxious," *Journal of Experimental Social Psychology* 42 (September 2006): 694.

7. Carey W. Sherman, Noah J. Webster, and Toni C. Antonucci, "Dementia Caregiving in the Context of Late-Life Remarriage: Support Networks, Relationship Quality, and Well-Being," *Journal of Marriage and Family* 75 (October 2013): 1157.

8. Pew Research Center, *A Portrait of Stepfamilies*, January 13, 2011, http://www.pewsocialtrends.org/2011/01/13/a-portrait-of-stepfamilies/.

CHAPTER 19: CONSTRUCT
HEALTHY BOUNDARIES

1. Constance Ahrons, *The Good Divorce* (New York: HarperCollins, 1994), 6.

CHAPTER 20: BALANCE POWER
IN YOUR RELATIONSHIP

1. Pepper Schwartz, *Love between Equals: How Peer Marriage Really Works* (New York: Free Press, 1995), 15.

2. John Gottman and Nan Silver, *The Seven Principles for Making Marriage Work: A Practical Guide from the Country's Foremost Relationship Expert* (Vol. 2) (New York: Harmony, 2015), 116–18.

3. John Gottman et al., "Observing Gay, Lesbian and Heterosexual Couples' Relationships: Mathematical Modeling of Conflict Interaction," *Journal of Homosexuality* 45, no. 1 (October 2003): 87.

4. Carmen Knudson-Martin and Anne R. Mahoney, *Couples, Gender, and Power: Creating Change in Intimate Relationships* (New York: Springer, 2009), 354–55.

APPENDIX A: PETERSON AND SELIGMAN'S LIST
OF VIRTUES AND CHARACTER STRENGTHS

1. Christopher Peterson and Martin Seligman, *Character Strengths and Virtues: A Handbook and Classification* (Oxford, UK: Oxford University Press, 2004): 29–30.

BIBLIOGRAPHY

Ahrons, Constance. *The Good Divorce*. New York: HarperCollins, 1994.

Ainsworth, Mary D. Salter, and Silvia M. Bell. "Attachment, Exploration, and Separation: Illustrated by the Behavior of One-Year-Olds in a Strange Situation." *Child Development* 41 (March 1970): 49–67.

Alberts, Jess, and Angela Trethewey. "Love, Honor, and Thank." *Greater Good Magazine*. 2007. https://greatergood.berkeley.edu/article/item/love_honor_thank.

Aron, Arthur, Christina C. Norman, Elaine N. Aron, Colin McKenna, and Richard Heyman. "Couples' Shared Participation in Novel and Arousing Activities and Experienced Relationship Quality." *Journal of Personality and Social Psychology* 78 (March 2000): 273–83.

Bartlett, Monica Y., and David DeSteno. "Gratitude and Prosocial Behavior: Helping When It Costs You." *Psychological Science* 17, no. 4 (April 2006): 319–25.

Baumeister, Roy F., and Mark R. Leary. "The Need to Belong: Desire for Interpersonal Attachments as a Fundamental Human Motivation." *Psychological Bulletin* 117, no. 3 (May 1995): 497–529.

Bowlby, John. *Attachment and Loss, Vol. 1: Attachment*. New York: Basic Books, (1969) 1982.

Cacioppo, Stephanie, John P. Capitanio, and John T. Cacioppo. "Toward a Neurology of Loneliness." *Psychological Bulletin* 140, no. 6 (November 2014): 1464–504.

Carney, Dana R., Amy J. C. Cuddy, and Andy Yap. "Power Posing: Brief Nonverbal Displays Affect Neuroendocrine Levels and Risk Tolerance." *Psychological Science* 21 (September 2010): 1363–68.

———. "Review and Summary of Research on the Embodied Effects of Expansive (vs. Contractive) Nonverbal Displays." *Psychological Science* 26, no. 5 (April 2015): 657–63.

Chapman, Gary. *The Five Languages of Love*. Chicago: Northfield Publishing, 2015.

Coan, James A., Hillary S. Schaefer, and Richard J. Davidson. "Lending a Hand: Social Regulation of the Neural Response to Threat." *Psychological Science* 2, no. 12 (December 2006): 1032–39.

Debrot, Anik, Dominik Schoebi, Meinrad Perrez, and Andrea B. Horn. "Touch as an Interpersonal Emotion Regulation Process in Couples' Daily Lives: The Mediating Role of Psychological Intimacy." *Personality and Social Psychology Bulletin* 39, no. 10 (July 2013): 1373–85.

Elabd, Christian, Wendy Cousin, Pavan Upadhyayula, Marc S. Choolijian, Ju Li, Sunny Kung, Kevin P. Jiang, and Irina M. Conboy. "Oxytocin Is an Age-Specific Circulating Hormone That Is Necessary for Muscle Maintenance and Regeneration." *Nature Communications* 5 (June 2014): 4082.

Emmons, Robert A., and Kevin E. McCullough. "Counting Blessings versus Burdens: An Experimental Investigation of Gratitude and Subjective Well-Being in Daily Life." *Journal of Personality and Social Psychology* 84, no. 2 (February 2003): 377–89.

Epstein, Robert, Regina Warfel, James Johnson, Rachel Smith, and Paul McKinney. "Which Relationship Skills Count Most?" *Journal of Couple and Relationship Therapy* 12 (October 2013): 297–313.

Farrell, Allison K., Jeffrey A. Simpson, Nickola C. Overall, and Sandra L. Shallcross. "Buffering the Responses of Avoidantly Attached Romantic Partners in Strain Test Situations." *Journal of Family Psychology* 30 (February 2016): 580–91.

Feeney, Brooke C., and Roxanne L. Thrush. "Relationship Influences on Exploration in Adulthood: The Characteristics and Function of a Secure Base." *Journal of Personality and Social Psychology* 98 (January 2010): 57–76.

Fraley, R. Chris, Niels G. Waller, and Kelly A. Brennan. "An Item-Response Theory Analysis of Self-Report Measures of Adult Attachment." *Journal of Personality and Social Psychology* 78 (February 2000): 350–65.

Fredrickson, Barbara L., Kevin A. Cohn, Kimberly A. Coffey, Jolynn Pek, and Sandra M. Finkel. "Open Hearts Build Lives: Positive Emotions, Induced through Loving-Kindness Meditation, Build Consequential Personal Resources." *Journal of Personality and Social Psychology* 95, no. 5 (November 2008): 1045–62.

Gable, Shelly L., Courtney L. Gosnell, Natalya C. Maisel, and Amy Strachman. "Safely Testing the Alarm: Close Others' Responses to Personal Positive Events." *Journal of Personality and Social Psychology* 103, no. 6 (August 2012): 963–81.

Ganong, Lawrence, and Marilyn Coleman. *Stepfamily Relationships: Development, Dynamics, and Intervention*. New York: Springer, 2004.

Garanzini, Salvatore, Alapaki Yee, John M. Gottman, Julie S. Gottman, Carrie Cole, Marisa Preciado, and Carolyn Jasculca. "Results of Gottman Method Couples Therapy with Gay and Lesbian Couples." *Journal of Marital and Family Therapy* 43, no. 4 (October 2017): 674–84.

Gottman, John, and Joan DeClaire. *The Relationship Cure: A 5 Step Guide to Strengthening Your Marriage, Family, and Friendships*. New York: Three Rivers Press, 2002.

Gottman, John, Julie S. Gottman, and Joan DeClaire. *10 Lessons to Transform Your Marriage: America's Love Lab Experts Share Their Strategies for Strengthening Your Relationship*. New York: Crown, 2006.

Gottman, John, Robert W. Levenson, Catherine Swanson, Kristin Swanson, Rebecca Tyler, and Dan Yoshimoto. "Observing Gay, Lesbian and Heterosexual Couples' Relationships: Mathematical Modeling of Conflict Interaction." *Journal of Homosexuality* 45, no. 1 (October 2003): 65–91.

Gottman, John, and Nan Silver. *Why Marriages Succeed or Fail and How You Can Make Yours Last*. New York: Simon and Schuster, 1995.

———. *The Seven Principles for Making Marriage Work: A Practical Guide from the Country's Foremost Relationship Expert* (Vol. 2). New York: Harmony, 2015.

Hazan, Cindy, and Phillip R. Shaver. "Romantic Love Conceptualized as an Attachment Process." *Journal of Personality and Social Psychology* 52 (March 1987): 511–24.

———. "Love and Work: An Attachment-Theoretical Perspective." *Journal of Personality and Social Psychology* 59 (August 1990): 270–80.

Hetherington, E. Mavis, and John Kelly. *For Better or Worse: Divorce Reconsidered*. New York: W.W. Norton, 2002.

Holt-Lunstad, Julianne, Timothy B. Smith, Mark Baker, Tyler Harris, and David Stephenson. "Loneliness and Social Isolation as Risk Factors for Mortality: A Meta-analytic Review." *Perspectives on Psychological Science* 10, no. 2 (March 2015): 227–37.

Johnson, Sue. *Hold Me Tight: Seven Conversations for a Lifetime of Love*. New York: Little, Brown and Company, 2008.

———. *Love Sense: The Revolutionary New Science of Romantic Relationships*. New York: Little, Brown and Company, 2013.

Johnson, Susan M., Melissa B. Moser, Lane Beckes, Andra Smith, Tracy Dalgleish, Rebecca Halchuk, Karen Hasselmo, Paul S. Greenman, Zul Merali, and James A. Coan. "Soothing the Threatened Brain: Leveraging Contact Comfort with Emotionally Focused Therapy." 2013: *PLoS ONE* 8(11): e79314. doi:10.1371/journal.pone.0079314.

Kabat-Zinn, Jon. *Wherever You Go, There You Are*. New York: Hachette Books, 2005.

Kappes, Andreas, and Tali Sharot. "The Automatic Nature of Motivated Belief Updating." *Behavioral Public Policy* (March 2018): 1–17.

Keng, Shian-Ling, Moira J. Smoski, and Clive J. Robins. "Effects of Mindfulness on Psychological Health: A Review of Empirical Studies." *Clinical Psychology Review* 31, no. 6 (August 2011): 1041–56.

Knudson-Martin, Carmen, and Anne R. Mahoney. *Couples, Gender, and Power: Creating Change in Intimate Relationships.* New York: Springer, 2009.

Laurent, Heidemarie K., and Sally I. Powers. "Social-Cognitive Predictors of Hypothalamic-Pituitary-Adrenal Reactivity to Interpersonal Conflict in Emerging Adult Couples." *Journal of Social and Personal Relationships* 23, no. 5 (October 2006): 703–20.

———. "Emotion Regulation in Emerging Adult Couples: Temperament, Attachment, and HPA Response to Conflict." *Biological Psychology* 76, nos. 1–2 (September 2007): 61–71.

Main, Mary, and Erik Hesse. "Parents' Unresolved Traumatic Experiences Are Related to Infant Disorganized Attachment Status: Is Frightened and/or Frightening Parental Behavior the Linking Mechanism?" In *Attachment in the Preschool Years: Theory, Research and Intervention*, edited by M. Greenberg, D. Cicchetti, and E. M. Cummings, 161–84. Chicago: University of Chicago Press, 1990.

Mikulincer, Mario, and Phillip R. Shaver. *Attachment in Adulthood: Structure, Dynamics, and Change.* New York: Guilford Press, 2007.

Orbuch, Terri L. 2012. *Finding Love Again: 6 Simple Steps to a New and Happy Relationship.* Naperville, IL: Sourcebooks Casablanca.

Overall, Nickola C., Jeffrey A. Simpson, and Helena Struthers. "Buffering Attachment-Related Avoidance: Softening Emotional and Behavioral Defenses during Conflict Discussions." *Journal of Personality and Social Psychology* 104, no. 5 (August 2013): 854–71.

Peterson, Christopher, and Martin E. P. Seligman. *Character Strengths and Virtues: A Handbook and Classification.* Oxford, UK: Oxford University Press, 2004.

Pew Research Center. *A Portrait of Stepfamilies.* January 13, 2011. http://www.pewsocialtrends.org/2011/01/13/a-portrait-of-stepfamilies/.

———. *Parenting in America: Outlook, Worries, Aspirations Are Strongly Linked to Financial Situation.* December 17, 2015. http://www.pewsocialtrends.org/2015/12/17/parenting-in-america/.

Ranehill, Eva, Anna Dreber, Magnus Johannesson, Susanne Leiberg, Sunhae Sul, and Roberto A. Weber. "Assessing the Robustness of Power Posing: No Effect on Hormones and Risk Tolerance in a Large Sample of Men and Women." *Psychological Science* 26, no. 5 (May 2015): 653–56.

Salvatore, Jessica E., Sally I. Kuo, Ryan D. Steele, Jeffrey A. Simpson, and W. Andrew Collins. "Recovering from Conflict in Romantic Relationships: A Developmental Perspective." *Psychological Science* 22 (March 2011): 376–83.

Schumann, Karina. "Does Love Mean Never Having to Say You're Sorry? Associations between Relationship Satisfaction, Perceived Apology Sincerity, and Forgiveness." *Journal of Social and Personal Relationships* 29 (June 2012): 997–1010.

———. "An Affirmed Self and a Better Apology: The Effect of Self-Affirmation on Transgressors' Responses to Victims." *Journal of Experimental Social Psychology* 54 (September 2014): 89–96.

Schwartz, Pepper. *Love between Equals: How Peer Marriage Really Works*. New York: First Free Press, 1995.

Seider, Benjamin, Gilad Hirschberger, Kristin L. Nelson, and Robert W. Levenson. "We Can Work It Out: Age Differences in Relational Pronouns, Physiology, and Behavior in Marital Conflict." *Psychology and Aging* 24, no. 3 (September 2009): 604–13.

Shaver, Phillip R., and Mario Mikulincer. "Attachment Theory and Research: Resurrection of the Psychodynamic Approach to Personality." *Journal of Research in Personality* 39 (February 2005): 22–45.

Sherman, Carey W., Noah J. Webster, and Toni C. Antonucci. "Dementia Caregiving in the Context of Late-Life Remarriage: Support Networks, Relationship Quality, and Well-Being." *Journal of Marriage and Family* 75 (October 2013): 1149–63.

Simpson, Jeffrey A., and Nickola C. Overall. "Partner Buffering of Attachment Insecurity." *Current Directions in Psychological Science* 23 (February 2014): 54–59.

Simpson, Jeffrey A., and W. Steven Rholes. "Adult Attachment, Stress, and Romantic Relationships." *Current Opinion in Psychology* 13 (February 2017): 19–24.

Simpson, J. S., W. Steven Rholes, and Julia S. Nelligan. "Support Seeking and Support Giving within Couples in an Anxiety-Provoking Situation: The Role of Attachment Styles." *Journal of Personality and Social Psychology* 62 (January 1992): 434–46.

Simpson, Jeffrey A., Heike A. Winterheld, W. Steven Rholes, and M. Minda Oriña. "Working Models of Attachment and Reactions to Different Forms of Caregiving from Romantic Partners." *Journal of Personality and Social Psychology* 93 (September 2007): 466–77.

Smith, Emily Esfahani. "The Masters of Love." *The Atlantic*. June 12, 2014. https://www.theatlantic.com/health/archive/2014/06/happily-ever-after/372573/.

Wiebe, Stephanie, Susan M. Johnson, Melissa Burgess-Moser, Tracy Dalgleish, Marie France Lafontaine, and Giorgio Tasca. "Two-Year Follow-Up Outcomes in Emotionally Focused Couple Therapy: An Investigation of Relationship Satisfaction and Attachment Trajectories." *Journal of Marital and Family Therapy* 43, no. 2 (December 2016): 227–44.

Williams, Kipling D. "Ostracism." *Annual Review of Psychology* 58, 2007: 425–52.

———. "Ostracism: Effects of Being Excluded and Ignored." *Advances in Experimental Social Psychology* 41, 2009: 279–314.

———. "The Pain of Exclusion." *Scientific American Mind* 21 (January/February 2011): 30–37.

Williamson, Ian, Marti H. Gonzales, Sierra Fernandez, and Allison Williams. "Forgiveness Aversion: Developing a Motivational State Measure of Perceived Forgiveness Risks." *Motivation and Emotion* 38, no. 3 (June 2014): 378–400.

Wood, Alex M., Stephen Joseph, Joanna Lloyd, and Samuel Atkins. "Gratitude Influences Sleep Through the Mechanism of Pre-sleep Cognitions." *Journal of Psychosomatic Research* 66 (January 2009): 43–48.

Wood, Alex M., P. Alex Linley, John Maltby, Todd B. Kasden, and Robert Hurling. "Using Personal and Psychological Strengths Leads to Increases in Well-Being over Time: A Longitudinal Study and the Development of the Strengths Use Questionnaire." *Personality and Individual Differences* 50 (January 2011): 15–19.

Yackle, Kevin, Lindsay A. Schwarz, Kaiwen Kam, Jordan M. Sororkin, John R. Hugenard, Jack L. Feldman, Liqun Luo, and Mark A. Krasnow. "Breathing Control Center Neurons That Promote Arousal in Mice." *Science* 31, no. 6332 (March 2017): 1411–15.

Zadro, Lisa, Catherine Boland, and Rick Richardson. "How Long Does It Last? The Persistence of the Effects of Ostracism in the Socially Anxious." *Journal of Experimental Social Psychology* 42 (September 2006): 692–97.

Zheng, Michelle, Ryan Fehr, Kenneth Tai, Jayanth Narayanan, and Michelle Gelfand. "The Unburdening Effects of Forgiveness: Effects on Slant Perception and Jumping Height." *Social Psychological and Personality Science* 6 (December 2015): 431–38.

INDEX

ABOUT THE AUTHOR

Rachelle Katz, EdD, LMFT, is a licensed marriage and family therapist with more than 30 years of experience and the author of *The Happy Stepmother*, published in 2010. In addition to working with individuals and couples in her private practice, she coaches stepmothers and their partners, runs a monthly support group for stepmothers, and conducts workshops for stepcouples. She has appeared as a guest on several cable network shows and podcasts discussing stepfamily issues.

Rachelle received a BA. in psychology from Clark University, an MEd in counseling pychology from Boston College, an MA in clinical psychology from the New School for Social Research, and an EdD in family and community education from Teachers College, Columbia University. She is a clinical member of the American Association for Marriage and Family Therapy and the American Psychological Association.

Rachelle has been married for 28 years and has a 32-year-old stepdaughter. She and her husband live in New York City.